The Practitioner Inquiry Series

Marilyn Cochran-Smith and Susan L. Lytle, Series Editors

(continued)

Puzzling Moments, Teachable Moments

Practicing Teacher Research in Urban Classrooms

Cynthia Ballenger

Teachers College
Columbia University
New York and London

Published by Teachers College Press, 1234 Amsterdam Avenue, New York, NY 10027

The author wishes to acknowledge the following:

Chapter 3 was published in a different version in L. Pease-Alvarez & S. R. Schecter (Eds.) (2005), *Learning, Teaching and Community: Contributions of Situated and Participating Approaches to Educational Innovation*, Mahwah, NJ: Lawrence Erlbaum.

Chapter 6 was published in a different form in C. Ballenger (2004), "The Puzzling Child: Challenging Assumptions about Participation and Meaning in Talking Science," in *Language Arts, 81*(4).

Chapter 7 appeared in a different form in Z. F. Beykont (Ed.) (2000), *Lifting Every Voice: Pedagogy and Politics of Bilingualism*, Cambridge, MA: Harvard Education Publishing Group.

Chapter 8 includes some excerpts from Brookline Teacher Research Seminar (C. Ballenger, Ed., 2004), *Regarding Children's Words: Teacher Research on Language and Literacy*, New York: Teachers College Press.

Library of Congress Cataloging-in-Publication Data

Ballenger, Cynthia.
    Puzzling moments, teachable moments : practicing teacher research in urban classrooms / Cynthia Ballenger.
        p. cm. — (The practitioner inquiry series)
    Includes bibliographical references and index.
    ISBN 978-0-8077-4993-7 (pbk. : alk. paper) — ISBN 978-0-8077-4994-4 (hardcover : alk. paper) 1. Education, Urban—United States.   2. Action research in education—United States.   3. Children of immigrants—Education—United States.   4. Bilingual education—United States.   5. Science—Study and teaching—United States.   I. Title.
    LC5141.B35 2009
    378.1'98—dc22

                                                                                    20090200089

ISBN 978-0-8077-4993-7 (paperback)
ISBN 978-0-8077-4994-4 (hardcover)

Printed on acid-free paper

Manufactured in the United States of America

16   15   14   13   12   11   10   09   8   7   6   5   4   3   2   1

This book is dedicated to Jack,
whose support and belief made it
a pleasure to write this book,
and whose inability to fall for easy answers
informs every page.

Contents

Acknowledgments

I would like to thank the members of the Brookline Teacher Researcher Seminar and of the Chèche Konnen Seminar. These were two remarkable environments to think about learning and about teaching.

Beth Warren, Ann Rosebery, and Josiane Hudicourt-Barnes in particular created a supportive and exciting place at CKC that allowed for a singular experience of learning science and working in classrooms. I could never have written this book or enjoyed so much the experiences it recounts without them.

I have been extremely fortunate in the teachers with whom I have taught. I owe them a huge debt of gratitude. They are deeply interesting people to talk with about children; they create where they teach a culture committed to equity and to a true quest for knowledge. Many teacher-colleagues have offered ideas, talked over their thoughts and in some cases read drafts.

Marilyn Cochran-Smith and Susan Lytle were instrumental in getting this book written and published. I owe them a huge debt. I also received help from JoBeth Allen, Mary Bodwell, Leslie Brunetta and from my most critical readers—my grown-up children, Michael and Catherine, and my husband, Jack.

Puzzling Moments, Teachable Moments

Introduction

"Our kids don't have the cognitive skills, they are not developed as much. They don't know how to summarize, analyze. I am not saying they don't have the ability. They are coming from a different socio-economic background. It's not realistic for us to have the same expectations."

—Bilingual teacher, Boston, MA, quoted in
Josiane Hudicourt-Barnes, "Our Kids Can't"

In a graduate school class, a group of teachers who taught urban immigrant children were watching a film of second graders from a wealthy suburban community. After watching these children develop science experiments and discuss their results, some of the teachers responded with some distress that their own students could not do the same level of work in science. It didn't seem possible to them that their students could talk and perform in comparable ways.

Various researchers have demonstrated the power of the language and thought of those children, poor, urban, immigrant and bilingual children, who do not traditionally excel in school (e.g., Au, 1980, Boggs, 1985; Gee, 1989; Heath, 1983; Hymes, 1996, Labov, 1972; Lee, 1993; Michaels, 1981, Smitherman, 1997). And yet in the routine practice of teaching it is often very difficult to see their strengths and how they are relevant to academic work. How can teachers bring this perspective more strongly into their practice? This book is an attempt to address this issue.

When we're using what we think are the best practices and they don't work for all children, we generally blame the child's background, often without even realizing it. We say, "The parents are too busy working to take him to museums," or "Her mother is too overwhelmed with the younger children," or "This child has too many worries to learn." We are trying to be kind. We're sorry he or she didn't have the advantages others have. We try to provide them. What I think this attitude does, however,

1

despite what are often good intentions, is take our attention away from a true stance of reflective practice. It takes us away from a stance before drawing any conclusions about the him or her inquires into the child's ideas and into our own. It presumes that our on-the-spot assessment of a child's thinking is complete and it presumes that we understand how to "see" learning and ability in all cases.

In this book I propose, rather, that we regard these children who are not doing well academically as "puzzling children." Instead of quickly categorizing such children and their ideas as needing help, we must stay with an attitude of puzzlement and inquiry. By maintaining this attitude, we may find that their ideas challenge some of our own and that our sense of what counts as relevant or useful approaches to new knowledge will grow as a result of working closely with the ideas of such children.

Teacher research, in the tradition that I will describe here, is an exploration into one's own practice and into the ideas of puzzling children as a part of teaching. I hope to show how the practices of teacher research can help us to recognize the intellectual power that exists in forms of talk and engagement that to many of us appear at first to be of little academic value. I hope to show how by giving children more room to talk, by probing their words and ideas with colleagues, by focusing in particular on those moments when children are taking unusual initiative, teachers can expand their own sense of what counts as useful thought and participation in schooling, and thus challenge in a continuing process the array of assumptions that constrain what school is, what learning is, and what it can be.

For example, listen to Rubens, a fourth-grade Haitian American boy who studied science with me one year. I had asked the children to name some things that were alive so that we could discuss whether the mold we were growing in the classroom qualified as alive. One child had included the moon on our list of living things. Rubens, in agreeing with her, made the following statement about the sun:

> If [the sun] wasn't alive, then the sun wouldn't light and we wouldn't have no light and all we'd have is dark nighttime and all we'd do is dreaming, dreaming, dreaming.

Rubens's contribution was immediately striking and resonant, but at the same time I was worrying about the conversation I had planned, and worrying also about his understanding. Did he really think the sun was alive? What did the other child think, the child who had said that the moon was alive?

Our task, as I see it and as I present it in this book, is to meditate on moments like this one, when children like Rubens appear to be wrong, or when they are humorous, make unexpected connections, or get confused and confuse us; our task is to meditate on these moments in order to give them the time to develop; and then the task is to meditate on them further in order to see the thought in them, the approach to knowing and the connections to academic and intellectual traditions. Why did Rubens say this? What was he doing with such a proposal? As it happened, Rubens used these ideas to develop a huge metaphoric space in which to think about cycles of life and death, day and night, light and dark; his idea of cycles and their importance motivated the entire class in a way I never could have during the science we studied that year. (See Chapter 1).

My goal in this book is to challenge the assumption that children like Rubens—whose families have less formal education and read fewer or no storybooks and talk less with their children about school-like topics—have fewer of what we might call "intellectual" or academically relevant experiences. Their experiences have been rich and relevant. Their facility with language is fully adequate. They have been thinking and arguing, asking questions, and making sense. It is, rather, our own sense of what intellectual talk and engagement might look like that has become narrow and conventional. I hope to show the connections between the approaches of these children and those of relevant and powerful intellectual traditions. These children, indeed all children, but particularly children who are puzzling in the way Rubens often was, have the potential to reconnect us with a wider and deeper range of thinking, to the benefit of our teaching and our learning.

TEACHER RESEARCH

I am a reading specialist in a large urban school system. I teach children from a wide variety of backgrounds, from very privileged children whose parents had all the formal education the United States has to offer, to recent immigrants whose parents never had the opportunity to go to school, and many other children in between.

I was fortunate to have been for many years a member of first one, and then a second, teacher-researcher group. The Brookline Teacher Researcher

Seminar, founded in 1988, met weekly for close to 10 years. It was made up of elementary school teachers and also, some years, university professors with specialties in language and culture (Brookline Teacher Researcher Seminar [BTRS], 2004). Later, I was a staff member, and then, after I returned to teaching, a teacher member, of the Chèche Konnen Center (CKC) Seminar. Both these groups were committed to the principle that teachers learn from sharing their practice and exploring their students' ideas. Although I know that there are many approaches to teacher research, it is the practices developed in the BTRS and the CKC that I will be describing here.

This book includes examples of teacher research. It is also an instructional text with suggestions on how to do this kind of research as a part of teaching. There will be both narrative chapters and expository chapters. In the narrative chapters the reader will meet characters, children like Rubens and many others. These chapters focus on what children said and did and what I came to understand about that. They are often about what I learned as well as what the children discovered. These stories have one special characteristic. They include the children's own words. Because these research stories include the children's actual words, readers may notice things I did not, may disagree at various points, or may be struck by things different from what had caught my attention. Narratives such as these offer a degree of openness to new insights as well as criticism that is a crucial value of this kind of research.

And yet I am also often asked to talk in terms of practical strategies and analytical methods. How do you get kids to talk like that? How do you find their serious ideas in the confusing things that they say? Stories give a crucial feeling for the practice of teacher research, but they do not explicate in sufficient detail the rules and procedures and daily habits I have learned as a teacher-researcher myself and as a member of the wider teacher-researcher community. The expository chapters are an attempt to address this lack. In these chapters I will discuss the central practices of teacher research as I know it by describing the three following methodological ideas:

1. A focus on puzzling children and puzzling moments
2. Expanding the kinds of talk valued in the classroom
3. Ways to "stop time" in order to reflect on students' talk and ideas

What follows are brief introductions to these key practices that define this stance toward teaching and learning. They will then be described in greater detail and exemplified in the following chapters.

A FOCUS ON PUZZLING MOMENTS

The BTRS met weekly after school. Each week one member would be responsible for snack. I remember one day chatting before the meeting officially began, eating and complaining about the behavior of my students—I was teaching Haitian preschoolers at that time (see Ballenger, 1999; BTRS, 2004). I was saying how difficult their behavior was and how much trouble I had controlling it. I was trying to make people laugh, using extreme examples; I was very fond of the children, but at the same time I was exasperated. Sarah Michaels, a sociolinguist who was a member of the BTRS at that time, was listening, and I could dimly hear her saying, in counterpoint to me, how interesting this problem was. As I remember, it was like two competing choruses. I was punctuating the account of my day with exasperation, Sarah with interest.

Later I wondered what Sarah meant. Was what I had found so irritating actually interesting in some serious way? This was a turning point for me. These two different perspectives, hers and mine, in contact, helped me see what research could be. Research questions, I realized, weren't so much the ones I had encountered in graduate school, ones originating in theory; rather they were what I thought of as irritating or troublesome or funny—this was actually worthy of study, indeed in many cases these events were things we should feel compelled to study.

In the BTRS we came up with the term *puzzling moments* as a way to name these events. It is puzzling moments that we address in teacher research as I know it. They are moments when our plans for instruction were not being realized, when discussion went in unplanned directions, even when children appeared wrong or to not understand what we wanted. Understanding that the children were thinking hard in these sorts of moments was one of our first findings; this then led to a steady, ongoing effort to know what it was that they were thinking and how we could use their ideas in our curriculum. The narrative chapters in this book will exemplify what I mean.

EXPANDING THE TALK

Recognizing that there were children who "puzzled" us meant that we also accepted that the children were making sense, even if we didn't understand immediately. By calling the moments when they had failed to do what we expected *puzzling moments*, the BTRS learned to treat these events as "interesting," as something to think about and explore, rather than as simply irritating or distressing or something to correct or corral. It became a crucial tenet of BTRS practice that the child is always making sense. And this belief often led to a kind of stepping back when children began to talk. We were slower to think we understood what was meant and so we moved in less quickly and less often. We knew we needed to hear more. The children's talk expanded as the space for it grew. They talked more and the more children talked. The kinds of talk broadened; as we listened, we heard more jokes, more metaphors, more stories, more hesitations, more worries, more wild ideas, and just more. As teacher-researchers interested in talk and children's ideas, we now had a much larger and more complete sense of what children were thinking about. Our questions grew: What was the value of this range of talk and ideas? How did a child's joke help children learn an idea in science? How did a boy's story about helping his mother in her garden lead to a clearer definition of living things? Continually investigating this heterogeneous kind of talk, these puzzling moments, to find the power for learning and to support the connection with academic thought became the core of the teacher research I practice. I present examples of this kind of talk in various narrative chapters as well as in one expository chapter addressed to the question of how best to support it (Chapter 2).

STOPPING TIME

Vivian Paley says very succinctly what I hope this book demonstrates about the value of keeping a record of children's talk and ideas. She begins by explaining what she thought before she had such a record:

> I . . . wanted most of all to keep things moving with a minimum of distraction. It did not occur to me that the distractions might be the sounds of children thinking.

And then she reports the beginning of her development into a teacher-researcher:

> [With the aid of the tape recorder] the act of teaching became a daily search for the child's point of view accompanied by the sometimes unwelcome disclosure of my hidden attitudes. (Paley, 1986, pp. 122, 124)

As the BTRS came to accept that we were often puzzled by children's ideas, or even mistaken about them, we realized that we needed a way to reflect later on what the children had said so that we could take the time to understand. As we came to see the powerful thought in puzzling moments and in expanded talk, we realized that there was curriculum there if we could only grasp it. To reflect adequately on what was going on, alone and with the help of others, we needed a record of what was said. We needed to be able to do what we came to call *stop time*. Field notes and tape recordings became part of our practice. In the narrative chapters I will give examples of ways to stop time and explain the usefulness of doing so. In Chapter 5, I will provide practical advice on taping and field notes.

A NOTE ON SCIENCE

I work as a reading specialist in my school, as mentioned earlier, and yet most of the extended examples in this book come from teaching science. In fact, I include a good deal of science in my work with reluctant readers. Often I find that my students are eager and engaged with science books and activities, more than when reading stories. In some cases the science work described in this book was actually being done in a reading group, reading science books instead of novels. In other cases, I was teaching science not reading. In either case, I kept a focus on talk and text, and on science as a gatekeeping form of academic talk and literacy, something my puzzling students needed experience with in order to participate in academic life.

However, this is not intended as a book about teaching science. Rather, it is about seeing children thinking. How the world works is something all children think about, in science, in literature, in history, and in and out of school. Given the opportunity, all children can work with serious and complicated ideas and there is nothing like the thrill of thinking along with them.

THE CHILDREN

The stories I will tell in this book come from my own classroom and also from the classrooms of other teachers I knew and with whom I worked.

In the classrooms I describe in this book there are children who speak Spanish at home, others who speak Haitian Creole, others who speak

Portuguese and Cape Verdean Creole, and others who come from English-speaking families; some speak English as a native language although their parents do not. There are a few students who arrived in the United States barely having attended school before and unable to read. There are children whose parents were college educated in the countries they came from, or in this country, and others whose parents could not read or write well in any language.

Rubens was born in Haiti and arrived in the United States with his mother and siblings several years after his father had come to establish a place for them. Pierre arrived from Haiti at the age of 10 to join his mother, having rarely attended school before. Bernard was born here and spoke only English. His family was from the Azores; his parents had received a fourth-grade education there. Catarina had attended private schools in Brazil and arrived at the age of 8 literate in Portuguese. Her parents began by cleaning houses; after a few years, they owned a cleaning company. Djeissen's parents remained in Cape Verde while he lived here with an uncle. In addition to enrolling the children of many immigrant families and working families who hoped their children would go further in school than they were able to, both schools I discuss in this book were favored by many highly educated families with a special commitment to academic achievement and to diversity.

This book is dedicated to all these children. And in all honor to them, it is dedicated to the idea that in order to teach all children more effectively, teachers must develop their curiosity and puzzlement toward children's words and ideas, especially those words and ideas that strike us initially as less powerful and less thoughtful. The task of teacher research is to learn about teaching and learning from the point of view of what we are calling in this book *puzzling children*. The ultimate goal is to see deeply into the true possibilities of all our students and to find significant forms of engagement between them and what we are teaching. This is an inquiry that never ends. The techniques we use must keep us open to new answers, new responses, new children at all times.

THE CHAPTERS

Chapter 1, "If the Sun Wasn't Alive: The Study of Puzzling Moments, " is the story of the science talk that began with Rubens' statement about the sun. It tells the story of this puzzling moment and others that occurred in the same discussion. This chapter details the process of identifying puzzling moments, exploring them for the children's ideas and for their connections to various intellectual forms of explanation.

Chapter 2, "Expanding the Talk," is an expository chapter addressing the question of how to promote this kind of talk. It points to features of discussion that are characteristic of thoughtful and reflective conversation and strategies that help to establish it. Chapter 3, "Learning About Whales: Stories of Migration and Immigration," is the account of a small group of Haitian-American students in a reading group. As they read books about whales, they were often skeptical of this new information. In exploring these puzzling moments, I came to a new understanding of how the children were using their imaginations and their real-world knowledge in engaging with books on this subject matter. It is a study developed to a large extent in field notes and journaling.

Chapter 4, "Stopping Time," discusses some ways to collect children's words, using tape recording or note taking. Chapter 5, "Who Gets to Feel Scientific?" is the story of two girls, one whose intellectual strengths are easily seen and admired, and one who is usually quiet and appears to be slow to understand and to engage. This chapter describes a context in which they learn about science from each other. Chapter 6, "Making the Familiar Strange," describes analytical practices that help to uncover and explore children's ideas and concerns from what they say.

Chapter 7, "Vloop Vloop: Children Talk About Metamorphosis," is another account of a science talk. The children bring questions from their study of insect metamorphosis and ask them of their own growth and development. A detailed analysis of one child's participation addresses the question, What is Jean-Charles, a special education and bilingual child, learning in these animated and sometimes hilarious and even unruly conversations?

Chapter 8, "Keeping It Real," addresses two methodological principles of teacher research: how to find a good research question, and what is the role of context in seeking a good assessment of children's abilities. Chapter 9, "Djeissen's Question," is the extended account of a class of children following their classmate's question about the reasons for erosion in Cape Verde. It is a more complete story of what the children thought and did than the other narrative chapters. It demonstrates some of their particular strengths and how curriculum developed around them. Chapter 10, the conclusion, is a brief restatement of what I consider the most important principles of teaching research and teaching all children.

CHAPTER 1

If the Sun Wasn't Alive:
A Study of Puzzling Moments

The puzzle began with Rubens:

> If [the sun] wasn't alive, then the sun wouldn't light and we wouldn't have no light and all we'd have is dark nighttime and all we'd do is dreaming, dreaming, dreaming.

This is what Rubens, a fourth grade Haitian American boy, said to me. I had asked the children to name some things that were alive so that we could discuss whether the mold we were growing in the classroom qualified as alive. One child had included the moon on our list of living things. Rubens then, in agreeing with her, made the above statement about the sun.

This was a very puzzling moment for me. Did he really think the sun was alive? Did other children believe him? Should I correct him right away? These were among my initial concerns. In this chapter I will explore this and the other puzzling moments that ensued in this conversation and subsequent ones. Throughout I will be trying to describe how the focus on puzzling moments is an important strategy in teacher research. I will be explaining how this focus helped me to learn from and with the students who most worry me and how it also added to my understanding of teaching and of the topics we were studying.

OUR CLASSROOM

The students were all Haitian American third and fourth graders, some from the bilingual program and some from regular English-speaking classrooms. My colleagues and I had brought these children together because we felt that many of the Haitian children lacked some of the everyday information about science that the American middle-class children at the school usually had, such as how many planets there are, that water in puddles evaporates and then returns again as rain, that the earth spins on its axis, that whales are mammals as are we. Thus we saw some of our Haitian American children as having gaps in information. On the other hand, we had all seen these students work through many complex ideas in their conversations. And so, as part of my literacy work, I led periods of science talk and activity once or twice weekly and brought the Haitian students together for it in order to capitalize on their love of conversation, as well as to fill in some of the gaps in their knowledge.

I had planned on studying mold. We had put damp pieces of bread in various environments in the classroom—over the heat, by the drafty windows, in the light, in the dark. My goal for this activity was to create eventually some sort of representation, a graph of some kind, which I hoped the children would use to compare the amount of mold in each place. I also wanted them to explore and develop their ideas about what was alive and how we know, since mold is not a typical example of life.

As the talk began this day we noted that there was now, after a few days, more mold in every location. As the children presented their observations, they often used the word *grow*, saying, for example, that the mold had grown in this place more than in that. I asked them whether or not they thought it was alive. I was audiotaping this conversation, and a transcript was made that contains their response that day.

THE PROCESS OF TEACHER RESEARCH

I will go through the transcript in two cycles of reflections that are typical in my experience of the process of thinking in teacher research.

> Real Time: This cycle is analogous to the experience of being there. I'll present what the children said. I will annotate this first look with what I thought at the time, including my initial worries and confusion. I will identify the puzzling moments that I knew I needed to return to for further consideration.
> Stopping Time: The next cycle is the cycle of reflection. In reality reflection goes through many cycles. I may remember an event or a comment and understand something about it better or reinterpret it years later. However the initial period of reflection is what I will focus on in this chapter.

Eventually I had a transcript of this conversation for my reflection, but for a while in thinking about how to respond, I was working off my memory and notes and just the tape itself. Here, however, I will use the transcript to explore the puzzling moments, to reconsider my responses, and to better understand the ideas the students were presenting. I will then suggest in an abbreviated manner the kinds of curricular responses I made to the children's ideas.

In the final section of the chapter, I will discuss what I learned that might benefit other children, that is, what I learned more generally about how children talk and think.

PHASE ONE: THE DISCUSSION IN REAL TIME

Below is the text of the discussion. Note that participants could speak in whichever language they preferred, Haitian Creole or English. In transcribing the talk, I used italics when the words were said in Creole and regular print when the speaker spoke in English. When participants chose to speak in English they usually translated into Creole afterward for the children who didn't yet speak English; this translation is not included.

Brackets without content ([ ]) indicate that I took something out to make the utterance easier to follow or because the words were unintelligible. When I include words inside the brackets it is my best guess of what was said. Brackets containing parenthetical text signal translations and other interjections. Words in Creole are not italicized in dialogues. Curly brackets ({ }) contain information about what the speaker was doing while speaking. "CB" is me.

I follow each segment with a brief summary of what was said as a way to make the conversation easier to recall for the reader. I include my recollection of what I was thinking at the time as a part of this summary.

CB: Do you think the mold is alive?

RUBENS: I think it's alive cuz sometime it grow some, like, if you leave it too long, it's like it's just growing, [ ] it's like the bread is the mom, and then when you put the bread on the heat, and the bread gets hot, it's like, the mold is just born and then it start growing.

{Another child translates for Rubens, since the latter, like many of the mainstreamed children, claims he can no longer speak Creole.}

CB: So I think Rubens is saying, if something is alive it grows and it can be born.

RUBENS: Sometimes they dead.

CB: They can die later.

RUBENS: They can die like if you put it in a cold place.

Rubens says the mold is alive because it grows. To illustrate his idea, he uses a vivid metaphor, the bread is like the mom and the mold is a newborn baby. I restate for the class what I think his basic idea is by saying, "If something is alive it grows." I am trying to turn his way of saying things into a more general statement, a proposition about growth as characteristic of life. This seems natural to me. But what I said was of course not what he said, and so he responds with something more in line with what he was thinking: "Sometimes they dead." I was not expecting this and at the time I didn't really know what he meant. I was thinking about characteristics of living things, not about life and then death. I felt that he was being oddly concrete. I was thinking as I heard him, "Of course they die, but that's not important here."

CB: *Is this chair alive?*

KIDS: No.

CB: *How do you know that? What do you know that's living?* What do you know that's living?

{Children list things that are alive.}

SORAILLA: *The moon.*

Sorailla was a new student, recently arrived from Haiti. She had rarely been to school before. And this was a fairly abstract question. It was probably not one she had encountered in her school in Haiti, where things are usually done in very traditional ways. I was glad she was participating. But what could she mean? I was entirely puzzled.

Rubens and Michel, however, take it up very thoughtfully.

RUBENS: You see it in the sky.

MICHEL: It's always bright.

CB: It's always bright?

{I speak hesitantly. I am very puzzled.}

MICHEL: And when the sun goes down it comes back.

CB: Let's think of some other things that we know are living and we'll come back [later] to whether the moon is alive.

These two boys seem to be pleased that the discussion now includes the moon. And then Michel adds the sun. However, I am not comfortable with this direction. I try to corral the conversation back on track.

> DANIEL: Fish.
> {Rubens shakes his head in disagreement.}
> CB: You don't agree with him?
> RUBENS: I agree with him, but some of them are dead.

Daniel suggests fish to add to our list of living things, but Rubens shakes his head as if to disagree. Surprised, I question him: "You don't agree with Daniel [that fish are alive]?" Rubens again mentions death. And again I have no idea why he thinks this is important to say. It sounds random to me.

> SORAILLA: *Corn.*
> CB: *Corn, corn, what kind of corn? Corn you eat or corn when it's a plant?*
> SORAILLA: *Plant.*
> PIERRE: *Cayman.*
> SORAILLA: *Goat.*
> JOEL: *Animals.*

The children list more living things, using both languages. Sorailla offers "corn." I am glad to hear that she seems to be on track even to the point of distinguishing living corn plants from harvested corn. The list lengthens, and then Rubens comes in again.

> RUBENS: The sun plus the how do you call that stuff again?
> KIDS: [Various guesses.]
> RUBENS: Sea dragons, yes, they're born, they're far away from the sea. You know why, if it wasn't alive, then the sun wouldn't light and we wouldn't have no light and all we'd have is dark nighttime and all we'd do is dreaming, dreaming, dreaming.
> HERMIONE: Is the light alive too?
> RUBENS: This kind of light? {He waves his arms around the space near him.}
> {Hermione nods yes.}
> RUBENS: Yeah, if the sun is alive, the light is alive. The cloud is alive but you can't see it cuz it's vaporized.

[ ]
HERMIONE: But I see them outside.
RUBENS: Yeah, sometimes, but if you go on a airplane, to see it, you
    won't be able to.
FRANÇOIS: Last time I went on a airplane—
RUBENS: Can I just talk now, [ ] you can't see it [ ] and it's vapor.

Rubens is talking about brine shrimp eggs: You add water and
they seem to come to life. Then he returns to the sun and makes his very
poetic statement about dreaming and dark time. The field of interest ex-
pands still further as Hermione brings up light and Rubens introduces
clouds.

I'm very impressed with the unusual role Rubens is playing here—
the kids referring questions and comments to him—and I am impressed
with the serious and intense way they are all approaching the topic. At the
same time I am also worried. Do they know what life is? And what is
Rubens talking about?

In any case, it is at this point that I can tell that my plans for developing graphs of mold growth are not possible on this day. The question of
what life is and whether the sun and moon are alive is where we have to
go. We can't chart the growth of mold and compare the conditions for its
growth until we have spent some time discussing what it means to be alive.
I decide to put Rubens's idea center stage and find out who believes the
sun is alive and who doesn't:

CB: *Does everyone agree with Rubens when he says that the sun is alive?*
JOEL: No, I don't agree, because the sun can't grow.
RUBENS: Yeah, it grow.
JOEL: And clouds can't grow either.
{I ask Joel to translate for himself and he does.}
CB: I think Joel means that, what he said, everything that is alive
    grows. He doesn't think the sun is alive because it doesn't
    grow. So that means that everything that is living grows.

I restate what I think Joel is saying. In doing so, I have made Joel's
statement into more of a general rule, "Everything that is living grows."

Sorailla raises her hand and offers "elephant." She is still listing living things, working to participate in the discussion. A little later Fabiola
steps in (and remember, italics indicate Creole is being spoken):

I don't agree with what Joel said. He said that because the sun doesn't grow . . . It's not living because it doesn't grow. Some trees don't grow, does that mean they are not alive? Some people don't grow, they just stay short. *Shrimpy.*

We all laugh. She's making a sort of joke here. Notice she starts in Haitan Creole, changes to English, and then at the end returns to Creole and uses the Creole word for *shrimpy (ti rasi)*—not a scientific-sounding word in either language—to punctuate her joke. At the same time, of course, she is right—trees and other living things seem at some point to stop growing. She herself is a very short girl, pretty shrimpy, and she shows no sign of growing any further.

> CB: Yeah, they might be ti rasi [(shrimpy)], but do they just stay short, the same way as when they were born?
> FABIOLA: No.
> CB: So *they grow. They can grow a little bit. They can stay shrimpy, but they grow.*
> RUBENS: Yeah, they, they little.
> CB: I have an idea. I think if something is living, that means it can die.

I am thinking out loud. I have begun to participate just like the kids.

Rubens returns to the issue of growth for the sun and growth and death for the clouds.

> First for the sun and then for the clouds. You see, the way [ ] the sun grow is like sometimes when it's dark, don't you see, it's like a little bit. If you're looking for it, you will see the sun. Then it's dark, then it's dark, then you see a full sun. And plus for the clouds, when it's winter, if you go like {blows out his breath} and you see all the stuff that came out to be clouds too. They make part of the clouds. And plus, if you go home, and then you put, and you drop a little bit of water in a cup. And after, you come back. You won't see nothing and it's not going to be on the floor or anything. And that means it goes up. If you had a window open, the thing, it will spread out [ ]. And this is how cloud grows. When it grows, it grows, [ ] and after, when it starts rain, that's where some of [ ] the clouds die. They go back up [later].

I ask Michel to translate what Rubens has said for the newcomers, since Rubens himself always refuses to speak Creole. To my surprise, Rubens says he will do the translation himself and does.

This was a moment that I utterly did not expect. The sun grows as it rises, clouds grow from breath on cold days, and from evaporation, and rain is death. Rubens introduces his main example by placing his listeners in it ("if you go home") and clinches it dramatically ("you won't see nothing and it's not going to be on the floor or anything"). The audience seems to follow him, but I, at least, am quite surprised at where he takes us.

Then Hermione disagrees.

HERMIONE: Rubens said that the clouds grow, but it doesn't. It moves.

RUBENS: True, it moves, but don't you see when you go, {he blows} it goes up, it goes straight up.

HERMIONE: No, it goes this way {she moves her hands laterally}.

RUBENS: You can't see it when it blows.

FRANÇOIS: I don't agree with Rubens when he says the clouds grow, because what I think is, the clouds move but when it moves, I think it sticks together.

CB: *Can you say that in Creole?*

FRANÇOIS: *I don't agree with Rubens, but I agree with Hermione when she said*—how do you say clouds in Creole?

?: Nuwaj.

FRANÇOIS: *Clouds move, and then I think they stick to each other.*

CB: *They stick to each other?*

FRANÇOIS: Yeah.

Hermione is remembering things she has seen. She is not at all certain that when you blow to see your breath on a cold day, that breath goes straight up. François claims that clouds get bigger by joining together, not by growing the way we do.

Radine then tries a new tack:

RADINE: A question. When it's cold, you put water in the cold, when you come, when you look inside, I say it makes ice.

CB: It makes ice, so you are asking what makes ice? What do you think makes ice?

RADINE: The cold.

MICHEL: I agree with what Radine said.
CB: But do you agree with what Rubens said? Do you agree with what Rubens said, that the sun is alive?

Radine evidently wants to see how ice and melting would fit in with what we are discussing here, but I am afraid that the conversation will veer off in different directions if we address her idea. I remain anxious about the idea that the sun is alive. To me the idea of what's alive is the central question and so I try to focus the children there.

Pierre responds, however, with what is on his mind:

PIERRE: *I don't agree with Rubens. Rubens said that when you are standing outside, the sun is just getting bigger, when you are standing there, it's becoming bigger [ ]. But, when it's going down it gets bigger, when it's has to go down [(set)], it's getting bigger.*
CB: Bigger?
{I speak uncertainly. I am afraid I haven't understood.}
RUBENS: *I didn't say that. I didn't say that. When it's above it's big, when it goes down, it's small.*
PIERRE: *It is always big when it's going down. I used to see that in Haiti.*

Pierre is 10 years old and has barely ever been to school. He had recently arrived from Haiti and is just now learning to read and write. Pierre is disagreeing not about what is alive, but about the way the sun grows or the idea that it grows. Rubens had said that it first appears small and then gets bigger and bigger—a form of growing. Pierre says: "It is always big when it goes down. I used to see that in Haiti." Notice Rubens's speech is in italics; that is, he is speaking in Creole, although he often says he cannot.

I'm lost. I don't know what Pierre is talking about. I think he is not making sense. He is stumbling a bit as he speaks. And it makes sense to me that the sun appears a little and then a little more and a little more until it is big.

Fabiola, however, pipes up to say she agrees with Pierre, she has seen this on the bus going home from school. It *is* bigger as it sets. Up in the sky the light is all spread around and it changes color, she says. Then Rose agrees: "Yes, it changes color when it goes down." I am at sea.

Suddenly the kids have to go to lunch. They are late. Michel stays briefly. I'm desperate to get Michel on the right track, since I have the impression, from what he said earlier, that he still thinks that the sun is alive because it returns every day. I ask him if he thinks the sun is alive. He responds:

> It's not alive cuz it never dies. You know the question that you said, everything that is alive dies, I agree with that cuz if you plant a flower, and you don't put enough water, it'll die.

PHASE TWO: STOPPING TIME

At times this conversation had me thoroughly puzzled and worried and at other times I was exhilarated by the engagement and interest shown by the children. Often I couldn't understand what they meant or why they said what they did. This is the first part of teacher research as I practice it—trusting the children to be making sense, letting them continue and hoping you will understand more later. But then there comes the need to make sense of what they think and to both find and strengthen the connections to academic ideas.

In this section I will be using the transcript to explore further the moments I found puzzling and then to describe the sense I found in them as I reflected on them more carefully.

PM 1: "Sometimes they dead."

First, let us consider this remark in the beginning from Rubens. I said, "So I think Rubens is saying, if something is alive it grows and it can be born." Rubens replied, "Sometimes they dead." He returned to this point when Daniel has added fish to our list of things that are alive: "I agree, but sometimes they dead."

I heard the two remarks but I made no real sense of them at the time. After thinking about it, I now realize that Rubens was using a version of the term *living thing* that was different from mine. Living things and dead things are opposites to Rubens; but they were not opposites to me at that moment. I was seeing the world as composed of animate and inanimate things. Thinking in this way, I could have shown the class a perfectly dead fish and, pointing to its gills, used it to explain that living things have some way of exchanging gases with the outside. In other words, I could have described a dead fish as a living thing. Rubens was understandably wondering about this. I was not wrong, but neither was he. I was so focused on the biological distinction between animate and inanimate things that I didn't see that Rubens was thinking of life and death.

Some teachers might have anticipated this confusion; I know the science teacher at my school was familiar with it. But this was a classic puzzling moment for me, a kind of interaction that often happens to me. I find myself thinking that someone is fixed on an irrelevant detail, that he or she is being overly concrete in some way. Then later, I realize that the person was making good sense and I missed it because certain ideas are so strong, and organize the world so clearly for me, that I no longer see the ground level. I was comfortable with the concept of a living thing as an abstraction and so I forgot to probe what it might mean in an example from the real world. Is a dead fish a living thing or a dead thing? Or both?

PM 2: Sorailla includes the moon on our list of things that are alive.

I do not have much idea what she meant there. I didn't stop and let her tell us at the moment. With some children I would have asked them afterward what they meant so that I could include their thinking and also learn from it. Since Sorailla was a very nice arrival, and probably hadn't attended a great deal of school in Haiti, I think I had some sense that this was really all she could say and so I did not return to her. However, this was not a fair assumption and I should have tried to find out somehow what was behind her statement. It showed a lack of confidence in her that I now regret. She demonstrated later, when she offered "elephant" and "corn," that she was not so confused about living and nonliving as it had appeared. And it is worth noting that she was the first to mention a plant. This is further evidence that she must have meant something when she said, "Moon." If I hadn't listened again to the discussion on tape I would probably have remembered only that she had listed the moon as a living thing. I would have retained a sense that she did not really understand, when I think she did.

Still, it remains true that Sorailla said that the moon is alive. I continue to puzzle about why she would say this, and why others would take her up on it. As part of my reflective process on this puzzling moment, I have shared this incident with other people; when I have spoken about it with Haitian people, many have reminded me of how strong and vivid the moon looks in Haiti. One person told me about driving on a road in Haiti at night when the electricity went out, a very common occurrence, and the moon to her seemed so benign and helpful and the only thing full of light; from this experience, she said that it seemed almost reasonable to regard it as alive. Another woman, a teacher who lives now in the northeast United States, spoke of returning regularly to her home in South Carolina to visit her mother and sitting on the porch with her at night. They would watch the moon come up, and to this woman the moon and her mother felt somehow related in the comfort they offered her. The moon was like a friend or part of the family. So it seems that many of us have experienced feelings about the moon that contain a strong sense of emotional connection, not unlike what we feel for living things.

Recently I was observing in a seventh-grade science class where again the question of the characteristics of living things was being discussed. The children were playing a game in which the teacher mentioned something, a bird, a rock, the sun, and the children had to say whether it was living or nonliving; if it was nonliving, they had to mention one of the characteristics of life that was absent in that particular thing in order to support their claim. When the sun was called, a number of children said it was living. On their worksheets it seemed to me that they had classified it as nonliving, but in the game it came out differently. The discrepancy was passed over on this day and I don't know what they meant, but there it was again, this idea that there is some reason to consider the sun as living. Sorailla was not so completely off base as I had first thought. These other children also had something in mind that I do not fully understand.

PM 3: The moon and the sun and the clouds.

In the next puzzling moments other students, students who've been here longer than Sorailla, take up this idea that the moon is alive and expand it. It seemed to me at the time that Rubens, and a number of the other children, really thought that the sun was alive or were at least willing to entertain the idea. Let us address Michel's ideas and then Rubens's.

Michel responded to Sorailla:

MICHEL: It's always bright.
CB: It's always bright?
{I speak hesitantly. I am very puzzled.}
MICHEL: And when the sun goes down it comes back.

Michel's idea seemed to be that the sun may appear to be gone at night, but it always comes back. This reminds me of small children who fear that their mothers are never coming back when the mothers are out of sight.

When I taught in early childhood special education classes, I had a young student who feared that his mother was gone forever whenever he left her to come to school. We used to call her up so that he could realize that, even though she had disappeared from his view, she was still there. Michel seemed to be saying that when something that has gone reappears this is a kind of proof that it has not died and by extension is alive.

Rubens's initial statement seems a little different:

If [the sun] wasn't alive, then the sun wouldn't light and we wouldn't have no light and all we'd have is dark nighttime and all we'd do is dreaming, dreaming, dreaming.

He seemed to be thinking of light and life as connected, and darkness as connected to sleep, or even death.

Rubens a little later offered his explanation of growth and death for clouds:

And plus, if you go home, and then you put, and you drop a little bit of water in a cup. And after, you come back. You won't see nothing and it's not going to be on the floor or anything. And that means it goes up. If you had a window open, the thing, it will spread out [ ]. And this is how cloud grows. When it grows, it grows, [ ] and after, when it starts rain, that's where some of [ ] the clouds die. They go back up [later].

I believe that Rubens was trying to think about cycles and patterns from his first utterance. He was noticing the rhythms of light and dark, sleep and waking, and thinking about the sun's role in creating this rhythm. Then, when he turned to the clouds and the disappearance and eventual return of water in the water cycle, he was exploring another example of a sort of rhythm or pattern, which he again connected to death and life. Rubens and maybe some of the others seem to be playing in a huge metaphoric space. What is birth like? What is growth like? What is death like? How can a cycle help us to understand how things change?

PM 4: In this puzzling moment, Pierre made the general claim that the sun is always bigger when it is setting.

Because I had it written down, I later checked with others, who confirmed Pierre's observation. It is more obvious in Haiti perhaps, but it is also true where I live that the sun on the horizon appears very large. This has to do with the way the atmosphere, at its thickest, spreads the rays of sun. So I was completely wrong in this exchange as I disagreed with him, as did many of the Haitian American children. In our lives in the city, we don't see the sun on the horizon often.

And yet we have all seen it. I think even the city dwellers did know what Pierre told us, as Fabiola proved from her experience in the school bus, but for most of us something stood in the way of our recognition of Pierre's idea. We were tricked by our own sense of the logic of the situation—it must be a little bit smaller, a little bit smaller, and so on. We couldn't easily understand Pierre, because we were focusing on something else.

I think perhaps even without a tape recording I would have remembered this statement of Pierre's and eventually sorted out the truth of it, with the help of others. I learned from this experience how the context of schooling could cut me off from things I've seen, could cut me off to such an extent that, at least for a while, I couldn't figure out what a child meant.

PM 5: Radine wanted to know how freezing fits in with all this growth and death.

Again I did not understand this at the time. I was so concerned about the issue of what was alive that Radine's comment sounded to me like a random association. The idea that something is a random association is almost never accurate in my experience, but in the midst of discussion I continue to make assumptions that children might be doing this. Since I didn't understand her, I returned the conversation to Rubens's claim. I did not step back and let her elaborate here although later on in this study we did come back to the idea of ice and melting and she had her say.

CURRICULUM FOR THESE CHILDREN

During this period of reflection, of transcribing, telling parts of the story to others, thinking through the children's ideas, I developed a much more accurate and complex understanding of my students' thinking in this conversation. I could feel their interests and recognize some of the connections they were making. I also began to see areas of my own confusion. What to do next? I will give only a few examples of what we did, not as a model that others should follow, but just as possible responses to their energy and ideas.

First I changed the topic to the water cycle. I then looked closely at Rubens's thinking.

Rubens seemed to have come to the water cycle as a way to think about what growth or life could be for the sun or for clouds. He was imagining the sun and the clouds somehow, and he drew many other children into this. He had created a lot of motivation, a sort of feeling of mystery about the water cycle. Despite his unbiological claim—that the sun was alive and the clouds as well—he gave an impressive level of both dramatic and methodological detail in his argument:

> And plus, if you go home, and then you put, and you drop a little bit of water in a cup. And after, you come back. You won't see nothing and it's not going to be on the floor or anything. And that means it goes up. If you had a window open, the thing, it will spread out. And this is how cloud grows. When it grows, it grows, [ ] and after, when it starts rain, that's where some of the clouds die. They go back up [later].

This was so clearly suggestive of an experiment that I decided to set it up. The children and I watched cups of water evaporate on the heater, in the darkest and coldest parts of the classroom, and in the sunniest. We observed that, as he had claimed, the water evaporates away.

One day as we were measuring the remaining amounts of water in the cups, François raised a big question: Holding up the cup to demonstrate to the class that there was no hole in it, he asked, "But it didn't go down. How could it go up?" Until François's question we had been assuming that water evaporates up without really noticing that this was not something we truly understood. We had a science talk in which we made lists of things or creatures that can go up. The children's examples included birds, airplanes, fire, smoke, and steam.

I read them a book that stated that heat rises. This claim was probed and led to other questions: Why, if heat rises, are mountains cooler than lower ground? Does the water vapor go all the way to the sun?

Rubens's proposal that if the window is open, the water vapor will go up and join the clouds, led to much speculation about the opposite case: What happens to the water vapor when the window is not open? Why doesn't it rain in the classroom, or water condense on the ceiling?

The book also told them that there was water vapor, invisible, in the air all around them, and they enjoyed this idea immensely. They sprayed water into the air with the plant sprayer, or flicked water from their wet fingers, observing that it vanished into the air. But then they asked, How can it get together to form a drop of water? We made terraria out of plastic containers and plastic tops to take home. We put some soil with grass in them and each child took one. Soon enough the children reported that water vapor was forming big droplets on the top of their containers, although we still couldn't explain clearly how it was doing this. We sent children home to watch ice melt in a glass in response to Radine's topic and also to observe the condensation on the outside of the glass. We imagined and playacted how condensation might occur. We spent a great deal of time recalling experiences of our breath freezing in the water outside. We placed cups of water inside the freezer in school to see if water would evaporate there.

Since that year I think I have done a much better job of addressing the idea of condensation; I think that at that time I was only beginning to recognize from the children's questions how much I didn't know about it.

We tried to pursue Pierre's idea too, finding tools that allowed us to measure the orb of the sun without becoming confused by the halo of rays all around it. It never quite worked, but we did try. The process of trying to measure the orb seemed to somehow make it clear to the children that the sun was not changing its size, but was becoming visible.

The children worked in teams to draw big water-cycle diagrams. They then used these to explain what they knew to the kindergarten classes.

Rubens remained a leader, although he shared this role with many others. Interestingly, never again did anyone suggest that the sun or clouds or the moon was alive. As I will discuss in the conclusion to this chapter, this original puzzling moment may have provided an exciting and motivating feeling about the topic, but the students proceeded to distinguish biological growth from other, nonbiological ways of using the word *grow* and to learn the science of the water cycle in a way that did not create any confusion about what is conventionally considered living and nonliving.

IDEAS FOR OTHER CHILDREN

What did I learn from these children that will help me with other children? What might be of value in other classrooms?

First, I learned about the value of emotional and affective connections to subject matter from these children. Emotion is often absent from school science. There is a widespread impression that it is absent from science itself. My husband, when an undergraduate, took a course with a Nobel Prize–winning astronomer. This man, whose professional life was spent largely among the highly complex equations that make up the details of the laws of astrophysics, began the course by telling the students: If you want to take this course, first of all, you must love the stars. Of course scientific thinking requires objectivity, but my students and their highly vivid engagement reminded me that the drive and motivation to get involved with something must derive in part from an emotional connection, as my husband's professor suggested.

Rubens introduces the wonder of sea dragons that can be born far away from the sea. Their life—or their birth—is a mystery to him. Then he tells us that without the sun we couldn't live, or we could only dream. You can feel the emotion in these vivid ideas, about dreaming forever, the light of the sun, the connection between sun and life, between darkness and perhaps death. Then Hermione asks Rubens a question I would never have thought of: If the sun is alive, is the light alive? As attention turns to clouds, one feels that children are thinking about things that are very exciting— vaporized things, the sun, the living light, life and death. I think Rubens introduced a metaphor here—the changes in the sky can be compared to life and death and growth—and that this metaphor attracted many children to think with him. The metaphor, because it addressed important, fearful, and vivid concerns, also brought emotion into the conversation. I would probably have stopped it if they had allowed me to, and led them back to more prosaic thoughts.

Let me next consider their argumentative style and what they accomplish through it. What relation does their way of talking have to scientific thinking in general? Is this kind of arguing valuable for other children and other classrooms?

Joel begins one chain of agreement and disagreement by saying that neither the sun nor the clouds grow, and so they are not alive. Fabiola challenges this statement that everything that is alive must grow, by pointing out that some people and some trees don't grow always. Rubens comes back with his way of seeing cloud growth and sun growth. Daniel a little later shares his idea that although clouds move and then stick together, they do not truly "grow." And Pierre challenges the explanation Rubens gives for sun growth with the former's recollection of the sun's size on the horizon in Haiti. I was always surprised and charmed when such lively and occasionally humorous ways of discussing scientific ideas broke out.

I didn't expect this type of talk in science. With reflection, I can see that, through their back-and-forth argumentation, they succeeded in developing a much more explicit sense of what growth means in biology. The children recognize that although we can say that the sun grows in the sky as the dawn progresses, this is not a biological usage; and although we can say that the clouds grew during the afternoon, again this is not a biological usage. I think that they knew this in some way before; but making this sort of usage more explicit and stating it for themselves its importance in the context of this conversation seems to be both a pleasure and very useful as a scientific procedure.

Let me focus briefly on Fabiola's challenge. She challenges the idea that all living things grow. Her challenge seems to be based on what I have come to refer to as "the practice of taking extreme cases" to test a theory: If you're saying that all living things grow, let me find a living thing that does not, to test your generalization. Is Fabiola just fooling around, looking for a laugh? I am convinced that, on the contrary, she is issuing a serious and logical challenge. Not that she doesn't believe that living things generally grow, but, by using an extreme example, she is pushing us to speak more precisely. Furthermore, she uses the word *shrimpy* on purpose, I think, to make it clear that these academic terms, my rulelike way of connecting growth to a definition of life, have to answer to her common sense. But does Fabiola think she hasn't grown in her life? Not at all. When we point out to her that she and the trees have grown, she does not take it as a contradiction. She has made her point.

I noticed this practice of taking extreme examples first among Haitian children, perhaps because they do it with such rhetorical style and pleasure. But I have since realized that other children do it, too, and that scientists do it as well, as part of very sophisticated arguments. It is a good logical kind of challenge and one that is used in everyday arguing, on the playground, and elsewhere and also finds a place in the study of science.

With the feeling of serious playfulness in the conversation, many more children talked, including children who in other contexts rarely participate seriously or at all. There was more joking, more storytelling, more argument, even more Creole when they found it useful. Sometimes it seemed they were figuring things out as they spoke, for example, in Pierre's case, as he struggled to make public what he knew of sunset from Haiti. While I appreciated that they were using many more of the ways with words and much more the experience and thinking that they had practiced in the rest of their lives, still, at first I did not really recognize the value of this kind of talk. I kept thinking we needed to decide, one way or the other, whether the sun and moon were alive. Either/or. The kids—and it is regularly those kids who are not doing well who have the most to teach us in this regard— looked wrong to me, puzzling and different and not academic, and yet in the end, they helped me to wonder with them about ideas that were long familiar and had lost their mystery, to see the value of the new and novel connections they were making, to become curious about assumptions I had forgotten I had.

CHAPTER 2

Expanding the Talk

Among the regular concerns teachers have as part of their job is the disparity in who talks in class and how. Some children participate often and confidently. Others speak little and seem to be very shy. Some seem inarticulate or rarely to have the answers we are looking for. Others seem to be thinking about other things or to be mostly looking for laughs from the other children. When a child is not doing well in school, I believe, one of the first inquiries into what we might need to change should focus on that child as a talker and on the classroom as an environment for his or her talk.

This chapter is about animated and engaged discussion in general and how one might promote it, and it is about discussion in relation to children who aren't doing well and how different forms of discussion might bring them more fully to school. It is about what I learned from my own students—Rubens, François, Sorailla, and others whom you will meet in subsequent chapters—about hearing their important thoughts and their serious, and humorous, concerns.

THOUGHT AND LANGUAGE

Many observers have noted the linguistic skill that many children who don't perform well in school are able to demonstrate in less formal, less school-like contexts; on the playground puzzling children may argue using logic and evidence; often they joke and tell stories with considerable skill. Indeed, from the academic research on this topic it seems clear that in most cases these children are neither less articulate nor less thoughtful (Cazden, 1988; Foster, 1983; Heath, 1983; Labov, 1972; Lee, 1993; Philips, 1983; Warren, Ballenger, Ogonowski, Rosebery, & Hudicourt-Barnes, 2001). Instead I will argue that the problem they have in participating effectively in classroom work is in important ways related to the way we organize and evaluate talk in our classrooms (see also Ballenger, 1999; Gallas, 1995; Rizzuto, 2008; Sylvan, 1996 for some teachers' perspectives on this idea).

Courtney Cazden and Hugh Mehan first directed attention to the common format that teachers use for classroom discussion. They named this format for Initiation–Reply–Evaluation (IRE): the teacher initiates with a question, the child replies, the teacher evaluates the reply as adequate or not. Before the work of Cazden and Mehan, most teachers were hardly aware that they used this sequence, because it seemed so natural; it seemed to be the only way to do things. Cazden and Mehan brought to many of today's teachers tools to think about discussion structures and how they worked.

There are undoubtedly occasions for the IRE, occasions when it is useful and others when it is not. I do not propose that we do away with it. Rather, I propose that we be careful to regard no format as natural and that, instead, we continually develop our awareness of different discussion formats, how they work and, most crucially, whom they work for. I suggest we do this by keeping in mind the following questions:

1. Are all the children participating in thoughtful and reflective discussion in some aspect of the curriculum?
2. For the children I am most concerned about, what is characteristic of the discussions in which they in particular participate most thoughtfully?
3. What works as support and encouragement to promote thoughtful discussions of all kinds?

I don't think there are final answers to these questions. Rather, for me, asking these questions as I plan and assess my lessons is a way to keep in focus this aspect of teaching. With the first question I am trying to be certain that I am aware of each child's opportunities for participation. There are occasions when many children participate, but not the children I worry about, or others when many children participate, but mainly the ones I worry about and the others seem irritated. I am most concerned here with those children who do not show their skills easily in school, who are puzzling in one way or another. However, I do not mean to ignore the problem that can arise when a focus on these children leaves other children out. With the second question I am hoping to develop my understanding of the range of ways in which children talk as they are thinking, and to notice if various kinds of discussions affect who participates and what is learned.

And finally, I want to develop my awareness of what I do and how it does or does not support engaged discussion. In this chapter I will discus questions 2 and 3.

CHARACTERISTICS OF THOUGHTFUL TALK

Let me begin with question 2 by sharing here a number of things I have found in regard to the characteristics of discussions in which many children, including puzzling children, engage in a thoughtful manner. The most important thing that I continue to learn from "stopping time" when children are talking in school is that they are usually on topic. I may not understand what they are thinking at the time—I may think they are making jokes or wasting time, or that they are confused or need help, like Rubens when he suggested the sun was alive—but it usually turns out that they are thinking in constructive ways. When I have this principle in mind, I participate less and allow the children more room to explain themselves.

Douglas Barnes (1976) is a British educator interested in the features of successful instructional conversation. He points out that classroom conversations in which a lot of children speak thoughtfully are often characterized by what he calls a "first draft" quality. By this he means that the speaker may start and stop and hesitate because he or she is often figuring out things while speaking. There are moments in such conversations when words appear very slowly or in novel ways—these can be signs, not of confusion or error, but of developing ideas. When you are not used to it, you might believe that the speaker is unsure of him- or herself or needs help to be clearer.

At other times, however, almost the opposite is true. Conversations in which many children participate may sound like playground conversations. I have sometimes worried that the children were getting too silly and too excited. The playground quality has to do with a number of features: There is more joking, more storytelling, more argument in conversations in which many children participate. The students use much more of the "ways with words" (Au, 1980; Heath, 1983; Hudicourt-Barnes, 2003; Lee, 1993; Warren et al., 2001) that they have practiced in the rest of their lives; the bilingual children may use more of their first language when they find it useful. Logical and funny challenges like Fabiola's when she suggested that some living things don't grow but just stay "shrimpy," metaphors like Rubens's about life and death for the sun and for rain, rollicking conversations with action and drama (as shown by Jean-Charles and his classmates in their discussing insects and humans, to be covered in Chapter 7) are features typically more prevalent in out-of-school conversations; these ways of talking can function in powerful ways when they are introduced into classroom sense-making conversations.

The pitch of these conversations can become intense. I have noticed that this talk often contains emotion and imagination as well as information. Personal concerns may be brought into the classroom. For example, Rubens and Michel seemed to be talking about life and death as they discussed the sun and clouds. All the Haitian American children in my book group on whales (discussed in Chapter 3) became quite intent when the conversation turned to the place of Haiti in humpback migration. When a child brings up belief in God, or mentions his or her mother and her opinions or activities, I find that this is usually the entrée to a very serious comment or claim about our topic, whatever it may be. These conversations also may include what appear to be wrong answers or what we might think of as wrong turnings, unexpected connections, or what sound like random associations.

I have found that in these conversations students often take more responsibility for the direction of the conversation than is typical. There may be side conversations, in which children talk on the topic privately and without being called on. The children respond to each other. Overall I am less in charge. They push their ideas and often won't give up. For example, I was not able to maintain my agenda and discussion topic when the children began to discuss whether or not the sun and the clouds were alive.

Because of the nature of these conversations it is very useful to take notes or to have some other form of "stopping time," that is, of returning to what the children said in order to think it over later. The range of connections is, at times, very broad. There are times when a teacher may feel as if there's too much on the table. Remember that if you tape-record or take notes you can return to the conversation later and determine to your satisfaction if it was a useful intellectual activity. You can also make order of the ideas introduced and plan the next activity or discussion from what you see there.

SUPPORTING THOUGHTFUL CONVERSATIONS

Let me turn now to question 3. Here are a number of strategies that seem to support conversations in which many children participate fully and thoughtfully. These are based on practices developed in the Brookline Teacher Researcher Seminar (BTRS) and the Chèche Konnen Center Seminar (CKC).

Setting the Stage

In the BTRS and the CKC one commitment that we try to maintain is the belief that children are always making sense. Believing that the children are making sense leads us to see the times they are wrong or seem off topic or full of strange associations as thoughts nevertheless, and thus fertile ground for further work. In fact, if we believe that children are always making sense, I think we must pay special attention to a range of things we might otherwise either correct or ignore:

1. Jokes and laughter
2. Wrong answers
3. Side conversations
4. Apparent irrelevancies and flights of fancy
5. Stories from everyday life
6. Statements of ideas that seem to be obvious or well-known information
7. Metaphors or analogies of any kind

Such a commitment is not always held to in the moment, however; this commitment often means that we have to go back to a child and his or her idea another day when we have had time to think. Returning to a child's idea after having dismissed it or missed it the first time is really not a problem; the children seem even more impressed that their teacher is really thinking about the conversation and what they said.

Finding the Question

Many thoughtful and reflective conversations occur because they are organized around questions, real questions that someone in the group really wants to know. "Why do the roads in Cape Verde collapse and the roads here do not?" asks a Cape Verdean child. "Do plants grow *every* day, and can they feel themselves, asks a child who has been growing and measuring her own plant. "Is the Pledge of Allegiance a prayer?" asks a fourth grader from a secular family as we study Mayan religion. These may seem startling and impossible to answer at the same time, naïve and outside the organizing system of the curriculum, but they notably contain a real desire to know.

One way to start thoughtful discussions is to collect children's questions. As a CKC staff member, I worked with Marcia Pertuz, a third-grade teacher. Marcia wanted to engage her children in what we called "science talks," talks that would motivate the children, engage their thought and help them learn from each other. When she was starting out with science talks, she put up a piece of chart paper on which she would collect the children's questions. The children were engaged in many experiences in her hands-on science curriculum, so the questions usually arose from things they had all done together. Once a week one student would have the opportunity to choose a question from the chart paper for the entire class to have a talk about. One question the children became very engaged in was "Do plants grow every day?" The conversation that ensued is the subject of Chapter 5. The children's questions came from science for Pertuz, but they didn't have to. Questions could be collected and discussed from any area in which the children had some shared experiences.

Karen Hume, a sixth/seventh-grade teacher, describes a "knowledge wall" that she used; the children posted sticky notes with their questions on whatever topic the class was studying, and then, as inquiries proceeded on these and other questions, children could add comments, answers, and new information under the relevant question (Hume, 2001). The wall would typically get very full and complicated and so at various points they would write progress reports on particular questions and then begin again with further concerns.

In other cases the teacher herself might choose the question, focusing on some area in which he or she thinks the children are struggling, where they may be confused or confusing her, or saying puzzling things.

Another CKC teacher, Mary Dischino, puzzled over her students' responses to a chart the class was working on in mathematics. The chart contained the headings "Distance," "Kind of Movement," and "Speed." As children entered data into the chart from short "trips" they had taken in the classroom, it became clear that many of the students were convinced that running was a speed, while others regarded it as a kind of movement. Dischino was interested in why they thought this and how to help them see the chart in new ways. She ended up leading her class on 3 separate days to discuss the question "Is run a speed?" In this case, the teacher chose the question, but it arose from her genuine curiosity about the students' ideas (Monk, 2005).

At other times teachers try to choose questions that address big issues in a study, questions that will organize a series of discussions over a period of time. Suzanne Pothier, a CKC member, taught her first and second graders that the "big job" of plants was to develop seeds so that new plants could grow. Then as the children wondered about other things—what the roots did, the leaves and the flowers—their concerns were often framed as part of understanding how the plant did its "big job."

It also often happens that we don't plan our most engaging talks. Instead, we find the relevant questions as they are happening. In the statement "The sun is alive," the central question arose during a discussion in which I had other intentions. Chapter 7 tells part of the story of a discussion that began when a child was reading a science text aloud; as she read she developed a question about metamorphosis and human beings. When the teacher, Sylvio Hyppolite, heard the question and saw the reaction from the class, he changed his plans for that day. I think it is often the case that this kind of talk begins during something that has been planned as something else. However, many teachers who are just getting started with these kinds of conversations, as well as many experienced ones, find that Marcia Pertuz's system of collecting children's questions, maybe adding a few of your own, and choosing one a week to discuss is a good way to use the format.

Discussion Roles

When the questions come from the students, the teacher does not always know the answers, or even at some points exactly what the student means. On the other hand, when the teacher has chosen a question or topic, it should be because he or she finds the children's ideas around it puzzling or because she wants to hear what they think. Overall, the teacher is listening and trying to understand.

Thus these conversations have little of the IRE format, although IRE exchanges may happen for various reasons at moments during the conversation. When the teacher does participate it is as someone with another real opinion or idea or question. She may offer information—there is no prohibition against this—but at the same time, she participates with genuine curiosity, and many times confusion, about the children and about the ideas they are discussing. She may have goals for the conversation, but her curiosity causes her to remain flexible about the route to these goals.

Teachers make many different choices about the rules for children's participation in sense-making conversations. There are times when it seems useful for each child to take a turn as he or she goes around the circle. Such a structure has many advantages. However, it does not always allow children to respond right away to another's thought; each child must wait until his or her turn arrives, which may not be until after a number of intermediate speakers. The structure in which, first, children share their thoughts in pairs (Think-Pair-Share), and then the large-group discussion proceeds afterward, has the advantage of giving each child the opportunity to state his or her thoughts, even if only to one other child; it also serves as a practice run for many children who are shy and thus less comfortable speaking in front of the full group. At other times, a very open discussion structure seems the best way.

In some classrooms teachers have explored the question of who talks and who benefits if children aren't required to raise hands during discussions or if side conversations are allowed to break out sometimes. Some have found that otherwise quiet or disruptive children are comfortable with a more spontaneous format and talk more, and more thoughtfully. Often there is ebb and flow to discussions without hand raising, that is, a lot of cross talk and then, suddenly, only one speaker and everyone listening (see Hudicourt-Barnes, 2003). Sometimes the children seem to do this themselves; other times the teacher may decide to work on developing this sort of rhythm. The discussion on "Is the sun alive?" was largely student run. Occasionally hands were raised and children were called on, but in many cases children took the floor themselves.

Mary Rizzutto, a CKC teacher, has written that when she began with science talks she was particularly concerned that each child have a turn to say something; for this reason she used to go around the circle and hear from everyone. Now, while she still may do this on occasion, she feels that such a procedure can in some cases stop the flow of the thinking. She used to be extremely concerned about the quiet or silent children. She says she now is convinced that, although there are still quiet children she will need to check in with, it is important to allow the group ideas to develop in a natural way (Rizzutto, 2008).

There may be particular points in a project when a more open structure is useful and others when it is not. Students themselves may come up with some alternative structures that they can facilitate themselves. Whatever the rules, it seems useful for the teacher to model attention and to occasionally repeat children's words in a reflective tone. One form of this is called "revoicing," an idea originally described by Michaels and O'Connor (1993). Kim Alamar of the Whittier Science Inquiry Group finds revoicing very useful in her classrooms of Mexican American students. In her process of revoicing, she restates, in the same or similar words, what the child has just said, then gives the child the opportunity to accept or to correct what she, Kim, has said: "Is that why you meant?" she asks. Revoicing is often the main way in which Kim participates in discussions with her class. Doing this serves to slow the pace of talk and make it more thoughtful. It gives time and place for children to make themselves clear. It models respect for ideas. It also gives the teacher a minute to think, which can be very helpful. Further, Kim, who teaches mainly students who speak Spanish as a first language, believes that it is an important way to help her students hear their ideas said in more conventional English than they sometimes can manage.

In my experience it is not usually necessary to do much teaching about how to talk in this kind of discussion. The children generally seem able to agree and disagree, question and comment, without rules or direction as long as the question engages them. Of course, this too may vary and guidelines may be necessary, but I think it is a good, and challenging, practice to allow the conversation to be as much under the students' control as possible, which often means that it will be more like normal out-of-school conversation than usual. I think it is very worthwhile, as a part of teaching in this way, to continue to explore when it is useful to give students more control and when it is not.

WHEN DISCUSSIONS ARE NOT THOUGHTFUL

There are times when a question has been chosen carefully, and yet, when it is asked, only those children from the most academically enriched backgrounds raise their hands. There are also occasionally children who seem to think that they already know it all—and who consequently may make other children feel stupid. Or arguments can arise. I discuss in the following paragraphs a series of questions I ask myself when a class discussion has not elicited broad or reflective participation:

1. Was there a shared experience that I provided or that children had already had from which they could comment? When we ask children what

they already know about something, and they do not have a shared experience as a referent, they typically list facts, rather than wondering or making connections. Many children do not participate in such conversations on prior knowledge at all. On the other hand, reflecting on a shared experience can help children to focus on the complexity of an individual case. Everything you notice is somehow relevant. This may level the playing field between those who think they already know the answer and those who are coming to an experience to think.

2. Have we brought home experience into the conversation? Have we made it clear that these experiences from outside school or other formal settings are valid? I have noticed that many children seem to benefit from beginning with a conversation in which they can connect the topic to their homes and families. For example, once, early in a plant unit, I overheard many Haitian children mentioning the gardens they helped their mothers with in Haiti. We changed some plans and devoted a whole period to this—children drew their mothers' gardens and then presented their pictures to the class with an account of the work the children did there. Although this conversation was not closely related to the science we eventually did, it allowed for everyone to participate and it made it clear that information from home was taken seriously. This led to a steady stream of this sort of information, many of it highly relevant. I suspect that making these connections provides an affective environment that supports fuller participation. In all cases that I know of, it has been very helpful to the children when we create places in the conversation in which they can bring up their life outside school.

3. Do I need to teach them more before we begin to ask questions? Hume (2001) describes the difference between two classes of second graders that she had in succeeding years. The first group began with questions about water. Hume helped the children investigate these questions and, driven by their genuine desire to know, they had a very successful and exciting study. The second group had less experience and information about water. Hume had collected their initial questions as a way to start and she found that this particular year the questions were too broad and not based on connections with real experience. She has come to believe that there are times when she needs to teach the children in the beginning, give them experiences and information, and then collect the questions that arise and design ways to address them—she cannot always begin with questions.

4. Who was first to speak? I often find it important to carefully choose the first children to speak. The teacher may find that choosing a puzzling child, a child whose ideas will require reflection, will set a tone that helps other children realize what they do not know.

5. How was the question phrased? Eleanor Duckworth (1987) believes that "why" questions are in many cases less fruitful than others. Questions that focus more on observation and on how things happen are often more useful. The "why" is addressed more easily by means of these other questions.

6. Have I accepted a big word such as *gravity* or *viewpoint* or *independence* without exploring in detail what that word might mean? If the word is an important part of the study, we do best when we explore it in as many ways as we can think of; for example, we act it out, we imagine scenarios, we make webs that include many different usages. Again we take many connections from home experience. Afterward the participation becomes much more general and the ideas richer than that of just naming.

LEARNING FROM EACH OTHER

An important goal of these kinds of discussions is that children talk to each other and, in fact, learn from each other. Suzanne Pothier has developed a discussion structure that she calls "science workshop." These are discussions organized around a statement that was made by one of the children in the class. Suzanne collects the children's words during a discussion, usually by videotape. She then looks over the video with a colleague from CKC or by herself. She chooses something a child has said that she finds puzzling or resonant or interesting in some way. The following day she writes it in large print on chart paper so that her first and second graders can read it; and then she asks them, what does so-and-so mean? The ensuing discussion is often very rich. The children take the utterance as a starting point, articulating subtle aspects of the child's words and idea and then considering and reconsidering it in reference to their own experiences and ideas (Pothier, 1999).

Kim Alamar and Claudia Greene of the Whittier Inquiry Group do something analogous, which they call "the hot seat." This is when they choose a child, often a puzzling child, to explain to the class his or her theory about whatever they are studying. The other children are then engaged to figure out what the child's ideas mean. The entire group, with the focal child's participation, often both extends and clarifies the original thinking. The idea chosen is not necessarily a model of correct understanding, but is always the result of deep thinking. For example, these teachers once spent a good deal of time on the theory one child presented that the reason there is so much daylight in the Arctic Circle in the summer is because there are two suns. While this concept is not correct, she had thought hard to come up with it. It was the springboard for very complex and productive thinking about the sun and its path that led these fifth graders ultimately both to reach an accurate understanding and to recognize an error in their textbook's depiction. Kim and Claudia report that they have been unexpectedly successful in getting quiet, shy children to participate in "the hot seat."

These structures show children that they can learn from each other. They learn how to help each other to be clear and how to interpret other children's meanings.

FINAL THOUGHTS

These practices are exemplified in the narrative chapters. The initial commitment, that children are always making sense, is the crucial motivating belief that must keep us wondering about who is talking and who is not, our role in the conversation, and what other ways there might be to engage all children in the serious thought they are capable of.

CHAPTER 3

Learning About Whales:
Stories of Migration and Immigration

Field Note

Today I was telling the story of David, the one who killed Goliath with his slingshot, to my bilingual Haitian American fourth graders. After that event, David becomes the favorite of King Saul, but eventually Saul becomes jealous of David's fame and popularity. Saul in his jealousy goes rather crazy and he seeks, and evidently succeeds in, talking with Samuel, who is dead. When I reached this part of the story, my students suddenly got very excited. "Is this fiction?" they asked. Well, there's a question I'm not prepared to answer, I thought. Is the Bible fiction? Some say yes, some say no. The story of David and Saul is likely based on historical fact—talking with dead Samuel is probably not, in my opinion. As I tried to respond to all the different senses of fiction I suddenly saw looming before me, they told me that Jesse, a teacher at our school, had told them that their stories, of zombies and other fearsome things in Haiti, were fiction. They told me this with some small kind of aggressive affect, butting heads with Jesse maybe, but not so sure. Jesse, it seemed likely to me, and I think to them as well, was trying to protect them from what she regarded as superstition. Were they being dissed or not? They seemed to be asking.

I begin with this field note as another example of a puzzling moment. When they first said, "Is this fiction?" it had, to my ears, a school intonation—their use of the word *fiction* sounded as though they had a teacher's accent in their mouths, which struck me as funny. This whole interaction was funny. They had such energy and seriousness as they asked. And there was also my initial feeling of surprise, which was based on something like, Isn't it obvious when something is fiction? I had always thought it was. The entire incident was funny. I wrote it down and also told the story to various people to make them laugh.

Telling stories about my students to make people laugh is often for me the first step in coming to understand something new about them and about myself. As I hear myself tell the story, I come to understand it better. And people's various responses give me some distance and an awareness of my own expectations. In this case I could see that in this interaction *fiction* is not the technical and clear, unexciting word for my students that it has become for me. It is a live word for them. It is actively placing something in one category or the other. Particularly by relating the Old Testament story to the story about Jesse, they were showing me that, while the term has a definition, which they knew, how you see it in any particular case depends partly on who you are and what you are doing with it. Further, there was some discomfort toward Jesse. And yet there seemed to be some gratitude too. Neither the term nor their feeling about it seemed simple.

As part of my process of teaching and planning, I write down moments, moments filled with strange conviction, surprising intensity, unexpected connections, because I find it very rewarding to explore them further when I can think more reflectively. Doing so often shows me something about what the children find important or confusing in our work together. They can also be moments where cultural expectations clash—the children are expecting something from me that I don't deliver; I am expecting something from them and I get something else.

To simply correct the children, explain the word or the idea or my intention is something that, of course, I often do. And many times it works. But there are times when it does not seem possible to do this. The children won't accept the explanation for some reason. Or I am too surprised and puzzled by their response to try. This time, I did try to explain something about fiction, but I realized that I hadn't really understood what was behind their words, their engagement, their concern.

In this case, I kept the moment in my mind as a puzzle, until the following year—when it happened again.

It was my job as literacy teacher to smooth the transition from the bilingual class to the mainstream classrooms in whatever ways I could for my group of third and fourth graders. I was teaching a reading group and had chosen a book about whales because I knew that the children had less general information on this subject than did many of the other children in the school.

THE SIZE OF BABY WHALES

Field Note

*As we begin to read our first book about whales, the children read that
baby whales are bigger than elephants. No, says Abel, he doesn't believe it.
Vitale too has said she does not believe it. There is a chorus of disbelief.
Abel remonstrated that there are monsters pictured in the book (they are
included as examples of what people used to believe about life in the sea)
and so this book is fiction.*

Here it is again—this book is fiction, they claim, and with some of the same
energy. Many children will already have encountered ideas about the great
size of whales in books their parents read them, in dinner table conversation, in visits to museums. For my students, in contrast, this information is
new, and quite unbelievable. I disagree and try to explain why the book
has monsters and why we should trust this book, but generally I don't feel
I am very effective. I have said that I think the book is reliable; they have
said they think what the book is saying is not possible.

This was the start of an inquiry for me. The study began when I noticed for the second time this question, Is this fiction? and the seriousness
and force with which the children stated their views on what was true and
what wasn't. I didn't know very clearly what the study was about at this
early point, only that there was something interesting happening, something that they evidently thought was important.

My questions, as I began this study, were, What was going in these
funny, unexpected, surprising questions that they asked about truth and
fiction? What did they consider unbelievable? Was it different from what
I considered unbelievable? What do I take for granted and what do they?
And, perhaps most important, how do they, or I, come to believe something new? These questions weren't disinterested—interwoven in them was
my desire that they accept book knowledge, that they regard it with more
respect. I was quite concerned that they didn't seem to do this.

This chapter is not exactly an account of discovering answers to those
questions, although it partly is. More than that, though, it is an account of
teaching with those questions in mind.

So, as we studied whales, I set out to consider my students' concerns
about what is true and what is fiction. I took field notes as an everyday
part of my teaching and used them for my subsequent planning. I usually

audiotaped, although I didn't always manage to listen to the tapes until much later. Here I have pulled out all the incidents that seemed relevant to belief and fiction. As I present them, the reader will see that I included among them times when the students challenged the truth of something we read, but that I also noted times when I thought they were fantasizing, or speaking from imaginary worlds. I think that at the time I noted down these instances just because they were moments of high engagement, but I later realized that both kinds of events have to do with an attitude toward truth and knowledge. And, eventually, I came to see that the imagination was playing a crucial role in belief.

The following is the collection of incidents. They all come from the field notes and occasional tape recording I took in one novel group; this group took the question about truth and knowledge into everything the students read during this particular year. Here we'll look at only their study of whales. I will present each incident, or series of incidents, with some sense of what I thought at the time based on my field notes. And then I will again discuss each incident in relation to what I think now, having looked at the children's ideas throughout the whole study.

We read two books about whales. In addition we had a collection of others on the topic that individual children used to follow the questions they had. We made vocabulary cards for new words and tested each other on them as class began. We made lists and diagrams and wrote paragraphs, and we eventually developed a presentation of our work, which we took to the rest of the bilingual class. The following account is not a full picture of what we did as we studied whales, but rather is my account of their puzzling beliefs, as they stated them and as they changed them, and of the role of skepticism and imagination in their learning.

In this reading group I was, of course, concerned that they continue to develop their reading abilities, but at the same time, I had noticed various things among all these students that seemed to stand in the way of their being seen as more competent. One thing I had noticed was that they seemed to have difficulty with certain kinds of classifying. They didn't know that whales were mammals, which was perhaps easy to fix, but in addition they had trouble when questions about kinds of rocks, kinds of fish, were asked. I didn't collect any examples, so I'm not sure what precisely this difficulty really was. But I knew that this particular study had a number of possibilities for classification, such as mammals, baleen and toothed whales, humpbacks, and gray whales, and I planned to exploit them.

In elementary school we highlight the classification of the whale as a mammal. But, of course, for other purposes, for instance, a study of the ecology of an area of the ocean, the whale would be seen as part of a group including other creatures who dwell in that part of the sea. We say that whales are mammals and that means that they breathe air, they nurse their babies, and so on, but why we should group together animals because they breathe air or because they nurse their young is often left unexplained or just assumed. I didn't want the children to know that whales were mammals in the way I had understood it as a child, as an odd fact that was remembered mainly because it was so odd, rather than because there was any compelling sense beneath it. So I thought they should have some experience of the process of organizing animals into categories. We began working on the idea that there are creatures that have in common that they are born alive, and there are many others that are born from eggs. We were creating two lists of animals and putting animals on one list or the other.

WHALES AND EGGS

On this day I had told the students that whales are all born alive and that most creatures that are born alive are also mammals. I asked for examples of other creatures that are born alive and the children provided a list: dogs, horses, cats. Then Hervé suggested, "Birds." Radine remonstrated immediately, "Nan zè yo fèt [in eggs they are born]." Hervé exclaimed, "Oh, eggs? Eggs? How they feel in the egg?"

Hervé seemed to marvel. So did I—at his question. Radine responded to him with some exasperation, "How do you feel in your mother?"

Perhaps she was assuming that no one would be able to answer this question. Hervé, however, responded, "I remember."

"Do you remember?" I asked. I wanted to hear more.

Abel chimes in, "The [babies] feel good."

Hervé and Abel say they remember this. I am charmed, and puzzled. I make notes for reflection later and I go on. Our list now has two headings, one for animals born from eggs and one for animals born alive. I ask the children where in our list to place whales.

Hervé answers. He puts whales with the creatures born alive and tells me that the other list is animals that are born from eggs and that whales are mammals like horses and cats. I have a tape recording of this conversation and when listening to it later, I noted that he answered in a relaxed voice, but in a flat intonation with none of his usual verve. He knows I want him to get this classification business and he knows the answer I want and he provides it, but without a lot of excitement. I evaluate his answer: "Very good." I expect this to be the end of this interaction, but suddenly he comes back with a question for me. "How do you know?" he asks.

"How do I know?" I respond. "From the book. I haven't seen this."

How do I know? We have recently read this. What more is there to say? I thought to myself.

A few minutes later Vitale is answering the same question. (Whale) babies are born alive, she tells me, so we put them on that list. Again, there is a flat quality to her voice here. She is repeating what I have taught her. Hervé then jumps in excitedly. It is true, he assures me, "because when the whales are going, I see them big big big. No eggs like can . . . [be that big]."

Hervé's energy is back. Evidently he has been thinking about his question. Here he answers it, this time to his satisfaction. He claims to have seen how big whales are, presumably when they are born. At their size, he suggests, no egg could contain them. Our list is now verified by Hervé's personal experience, that is, by what he claims he has seen.

As I write more about this moment later on, I mention my sense that the students seem to grant little authority to texts, in this case and also earlier when we talked about the size of baby whales. Are they unfamiliar with this genre of book? I ask in my notes. Don't they know it's a science book? I have not seen the way in which whales are born myself, but I do not doubt that the book is correct. And I wonder, is this attitude toward books a cultural difference? It is certainly true that my culture is highly engaged with books. I use books to do everything from cook, to plan trips, to relax and enjoy myself. I know that for many of my students the only book in the house is a Bible, which is carefully placed out of reach of young children. I will return to this question later.

As I write my notes I also begin to wonder about something that hadn't occurred to me at the time: Is Hervé right that only relatively small newborns can be born in eggs?

What is going on here? Let us now look with some hindsight. In response to Radine's rhetorical and impatient question, Hervé and Abel claim that they know what if feels like inside a mother's stomach. Abel says the baby feels good but Hervé claims to remember himself at that stage. What is he doing when he makes such a claim? Is he being whimsical, which is what I thought at first? And perhaps lying a little in order to be persuasive, something I also thought?

After looking at the work the children did over time in various ways, I think Hervé means it. He is trying to remember and has the sense that he does. He also is trying to sense what it would be like for a bird, inside an egg. He thinks he must try to do this, since I am determined he know this. He is using his imagination as a way to come to understand. He doesn't accept information from books until he can imagine it himself. From this imagined experience—perhaps a very vivid one—it occurs to him to question how big eggs can be. He knows how big some whale babies are. Notice that this is no longer in doubt, even though he was part of the earlier challenge orchestrated the previous year by Abel.

Later I asked a biologist friend of mine what he thought about the issue of egg size and big babies and he told me that eggs provide nutrition and oxygen through a passive system. In other words, there is no circulatory system, as there is with creatures that have a placenta to pump important things like blood and oxygen around. Thus the size of an egg is severely limited. The air, for example, has to diffuse in through the eggshell and a large creature would have difficulty getting enough in this way. So Hervé's idea is not uninteresting. He didn't know all this, of course. But his intuition, based on his ability to put himself into these situations, is not wrong. In this case, Hervé helped us make a sort of visceral and biological sense of the difference between these forms of reproduction.

It is worth recalling here how the Nobel laureate James Black explained the ways in which he explored the structure of viruses. He has described how he would pretend to be a receptor molecule and imagine viruses coming to him, trying to figure out how to attach themselves to him. He claims that this imaginative thinking was crucial in his development of the drugs known as beta blockers. Like James Black, Hervé likes to get into phenomena and feel their experiences with them.

NURSING BABIES AND BELLY BUTTONS

During the following week we learn more about definitions and distinctions that are relevant to whales. The definition of mammals that we have from the dictionary tells us that mammals are the class of animals that all nurse their young. Vitale does some research on her own with one of our books about how whale babies are born and swim with their mothers. She brings to me a typed page one morning on which she has written that many whales live long lives and that they nurse their babies and care for them.

She explains to the others what the word *nurse* means, reminding them, with some impatience, of all the mothers and babies they have seen. To help the boys recall, she demonstrates briefly but authoritatively on her 10-year-old body how one nurses. Hervé tells us that he knew a man in Haiti who nursed a baby—he too tries to demonstrate—but this time no one believes him. Abel asks if boys can be mammals too.

Abel's question stopped me cold. It appears that in emphasizing the characteristic that mammals nurse their young, I came close to teaching him, and maybe the others too, that all mammals are female. So much for my interest in straightening out their ability to classify.

Abel's question is probably one I should have anticipated. It reminds me of how strange the language of these definitions is. The dictionary says: Mammals are the class of creatures that nurse their young. The *class* part is evidently supposed to make it clear that we are including both males and females, even though males don't actually nurse, but this is not obvious to everyone.

I reassure Abel that there are male mammals, and Vitale continues. She and Radine discuss where the baby is born from on the whale's body. They disagree with each other as they propose various fins as the site. Vitale claims to know from a book she has read. We have a book with us that helps, and as we look through it and read the text, the girls use their knowledge of babies and childbirth to realize that whales must have a belly button. Where is it? they ask me. I have no idea. I experience a moment of pure panic as I assure myself that whales must have belly buttons—they were born alive, after all; they must! Later that day I e-mail a friend who should know. He assures me that they do indeed have belly buttons.

TEETH AND BALEEN

My interest in classifying has also led me to try to make sure that the children recognize that there are different kinds of whales. So, in addition to our developing a sense of creatures born from eggs and creatures born alive, our classification tree now has another branch. We have divided whales into those with teeth and those with baleen. This is a major division for biologists in the category of whales. The children are interested in the baleen whales especially and how the baleen allows them to trap little shrimplike things called krill, which swim in, but can't swim out because of the way the baleen curves toward the inside of the whale's mouth. As I am walking down the hall with Hervé, he tells me he thinks that if a whale swallowed him, he could get away from the whales that have baleen, but not the toothed ones because he, unlike the tiny krill, could swim back out through the baleen. He goes on to explain to me how you can tell the baleen from the toothed whales. From looking at pictures in books, he has learned to distinguish these two kinds of whales by the shapes of their heads. He is perhaps imagining that someday he might need this information to keep himself safe. I am astonished. This visual distinction is not something I can make or even knew was possible.

What is going on in these last two incidents? Vitale is struck that whales nurse their babies. She is imagining, but she doesn't go as far afield as Hervé. Rather, she sticks to her own imagined future, as a mother, and the boys respond strongly enough that they feel excluded—they will never nurse a baby. Hervé in his distress imagines a solution: Men can nurse babies. Abel, while he doesn't accept this, nevertheless thinks about it in relation to the definition of mammals we have. Can boys at least be mammals? The girls continue to think about childbirth, which leads them to wonder about the belly button. This question caused turmoil in my brain because I knew it had to be true. Whales have placentas and live births and umbilical cords like humans, and yet I had never thought of it before. The whale's belly button is, as a friend of mine put it, a deeply conceptual detail, one in which one's whole understanding of the status of whales as mammals can be seen.

These students see details I don't see or haven't wondered about, the shapes of the heads of the two categories of whales, the belly buttons. These details are not unimportant. They are the details that constitute the classification system. The children are imagining in relation to what we are working on, imagining in the science, and they cause me to see the science again, reorganized and fresh, in their thinking.

ARE WHALES BORN NEAR HAITI?

This last long incident is different in some ways. Again the students dispute the truth. Again they imagine various scenes and place themselves in them in order to determine what could be, but here we also see most vividly how they work to put their lives in contact with school and with books.

We are reading a book about humpbacks. We come to text that says that humpback whales are born near the Dominican Republic and migrate up north each summer. "Do you know where the Dominican Republic is?" I ask. "Oh yes," the kids respond happily. "Right next to Haiti," I say. "Yeah, I know it," says Abel. "So this little whale was born right next to Haiti," I continue.

Suddenly there is an extended silence. No one says a word. Then I hear someone say under his breath, "Lying."

Radine then exclaims, "That's not true,{M kanpe, m pa t wè l [ ] Ayiti [I've stood there, I didn't see them [ ] Haiti}"

I reply, "I think it is true, ou pa t wè l men{you haven't seen it, but}."

They ask if I saw any whales when I was in Haiti, and I admit that I didn't.

Hervé asks, "Are you playing?"

"Playing?" I respond. "No way, it says here the little whale was born north of the Dominican Republic. I think it's true." I continue, "This book was made by the Smithsonian; that's a museum, so they tell the truth. This is a science book. It's made to teach you."

I was astonished when they challenged the idea of humpbacks being born near Haiti. I had no idea they would find that unbelievable. I again evidently decided that they didn't understand about the authority of science books, that this was a cultural difference between us. I hear myself on the tape saying, "You didn't see it, but." I don't go on. There just are things in books you haven't seen, I seem to be saying. Again I feel pushed to state that I believe the book and to invoke the authority of the Smithsonian. I am trying to be clear about how I understand the role of these books.

There is some sense of discomfort in this incident. Notice the term *lying* being used. They are polite children and it is later corrected to *playing* ("Are you playing?"), but they did begin with a more forceful term. I wonder what is bothering them so.

A little later on Hervé explains his thinking:

You know why I don't believe the story. [ ] There's no whales in Haiti, because I never saw one, every time with my mom I went to swim, cuz I know how to swim, I don't see whales.

He argues by saying he was there, swimming, and he did not see them. Hervé in fact can't swim—I know this because we are giving swimming lessons as part of gym at the YMCA—but he says he can. This time I don't return to my defense of the book. Rather, I explain why he and Radine might have missed them.

Maybe you weren't far enough out in the water. They're way, way out in the middle of the water.

Radine evidently finds this persuasive and reiterates for the others in Creole, "Yeah, they're not in the shallow water, they're way out deep."

I was distressed at first that again they'd rejected the information from a science book, but when Hervé sets the scene for me, I'm sucked in. I naturally place the whales for him and the others, in the ocean, but just beyond their view. We're imagining this together, something we often do as we work out how whales leap to smack the barnacles off their skin, or create nets of bubbles to trap fish. The tone in the group is somewhat more peaceful now, but I am still puzzled. What made them even consider not believing this, I wonder.

TAKE TWO

A few days later, we are discussing the term *migrate*, which the text used before when it claimed that humpbacks were born near Haiti and then migrate all the way up to Maine. Hearing it this time, Hervé asks calmly if it is true that whales are born near Haiti. He undoubtedly remembers that the books says so, and that I have said that I believe the book. When I say that it is true, Radine asks if I had seen any whales when I was there, a question she has already asked also. I say no, and again I suggest that they must have been too far out in the ocean. Abel agrees that he has never seen them on the beach. Hervé tells me you have to watch your back in Haiti, there are bad people there, he knows. He then goes on to list the generations of whale mothers born near Haiti. He rhythmically intones, "The mothers, the mothers' mothers, the grandmother's mothers," they have their babies where it is warm and then go north for food. This is a close, but more poetic, paraphrase of the words in the book. He seems to be seeing generations of migrating whales, over time, every year, babies and mothers on their way north from Haiti.

Everyone is listening peacefully and seems to find the idea of whales born near Haiti entirely sensible this time.

TALKING AND SINGING

The next day, Vitale, who hadn't weighed in on this question before, returns us to it. She says, "I saw whales in Haiti." Again, I doubt it, since she said nothing earlier about this. The conversation immediately takes off.

"Do they talk?" asks Radine of Vitale. Evidently since she has seen them, she should know. But then Radine answers her own question: "They do, all animals talk, I saw ants, *yon ravek ki mouri {a roach that died}*, all the ants went to him, some stayed but most went, so they talk." Radine has evidently read ahead, since the idea that whales communicate is on the next page of the book.

Abel says that birds go *eek eek*. Abel and Vitale mention other animal sounds. Hervé finds in the book the place where it describes the sounds whales make. He points to it and says the sounds mean "hurry up." We then read on the same page that whales can sing.

"I would sing every day," says Hervé.

They have no trouble believing that whales can sing.

Again they reject the text. Again Hervé includes a fanciful story, swimming with his mother. Radine as well as Vitale later claim they have stood on the beach in Haiti, scanning for whales. Then they ask for a repetition of the entire conversation. The kids end up spending time in three class periods stating and restating that humpbacks are born near Haiti. They were contentious at first, but in the two repetitions, they were quite peaceful. By the end the text is a participant with them, as they restate the part about grandmothers, read ahead about the sounds whales make.

What is going on here? Let's begin with the second repetition, the one initiated by Hervé. Why did Herve do this? The second time we go through this event, Hervé, content with the answer this time, warns me about watching my back in Haiti. Like many of these children, he may have seen some violence in Haiti, and he is perhaps remembering this as he warns me. This comment of his seemed quite odd and off track to me at the time—why should he mention bad guys in Haiti then?—but I now see it as evidence that he was imagining the situation in a good deal of its true detail. He accepts the book's claim about whales in Haiti and he's not sure what may turn out to be relevant. And at the same time, he wants to make clear that there are things he knows about beaches in Haiti too. Finally Hervé seems to almost celebrate his new comfort with this knowledge with his poem: mothers, mothers' mothers, grandmothers, all born in the warm water. This recounting seemed explicitly dreamy—he was clearly pretending and this time it is worth noting that his reference to Haiti is not about bad guys but as a warm and nurturing place. These final comments, to which the other children listen with pure attention, are resonant with the details of his own immigration story, and those of the others: leaving grandmothers, and warm weather, and even bad guys, to come north to grow up.

And then Vitale returns us to this issue a third time by saying that she was there and saw whales. I am reminded here of the conversation about fiction and David and Goliath and Haitian scary stories. Both these incidents have the same moments of discomfort in them. Both have to do with statements made by others about Haiti—Haitian stories as fiction, Haiti as a birthplace for humpbacks. It's as if the children are surprised to find that school is including information about Haiti. Haiti and their experience there have seemed discontinuous with school, and now here they are a part of it.

THOUGHTS ON CULTURE AND DIFFERENCE

Let us return to my initial questions. Did they really not believe the books? Was this some difference that came from the few books in their homes and from their culture in other ways? Haitian culture values challenge and skepticism in many ways. Was this a cultural difference related to that theme? At various times I thought that these puzzling moments were the result of different cultural attitudes toward literate authority, although that was never all that I thought about these responses. Now I don't think so or at least what I think is important about these moments is not that. Seeing differences in this dichotomous fashion—they do this, while in contrast, I do that—is regularly a stage in the process of understanding puzzling behavior in multicultural contexts, but I think this form of understanding doesn't necessarily help us to understand better what it is that we do so easily, nor does it help us to take seriously what others do that we don't. Once I find that I have come to such dichotomies, I think it is valuable to turn my questions around. The questions I began with focused on how we, my Haitian students and I, are different. At this point, for a deeper understanding, I need to explore how we are similar. This practice certainly does not deny cultural differences. But it does insist that we try to understand the puzzling things students do as a part of the range of human responses to new ideas.

Thus my questions became (1) In what ways do they treat books with belief? and (2) Where do I respond with skepticism and then imagination to other people's statements and claims?

In thinking about the children's response to books from the perspective of respect for literate authority, I think we can see that they were trying very hard to make sense of these claims because they felt they were important. But they had higher standards of belief than I anticipated. They were expecting to know things deeply, to make their knowledge a part of their lives, the way Hervé "knew" the book was right about whales being born alive, not in eggs; the way Hervé knew about the humpback's migration in the end; the way Vitale and Radine saw the whale belly buttons in their minds and then searched for them in the pictures. They didn't expect to just accept the knowledge being presented to them. They weren't just accumulating information, but wanted to be able to see through it. Their respect for books, one could say, was enormous. And this is where I think they have something to offer all children. Many of the children of the educated middle class, my own children, for example, are so accustomed to books and booklike information from their parents that they forget to take such material truly seriously. While these children believe books easily, what does such belief mean if it doesn't come into contact with other beliefs? The intellectual atmosphere that these students bring to our classrooms, or that they can bring, would help everyone learn.

Where do I respond with skepticism toward authority, and then imagined engagement? I worried many friends and colleagues about this, asking them if they could think of situations in which they had felt something similar to what my students seemed to have felt. A colleague mentioned the highly skeptical response of many student teachers when they are presented with forms of child-centered pedagogy they are to adopt. They begin with a sort of disbelief, she said, and then, to be successful, they must in some fashion reimagine themselves and their students in a way to incorporate this new practice. Or consider the response upon receiving a diagnosis of a disease. The hearer begins with a kind of disbelief—"This can't be true. It is not a description of me and my life"—and then is forced to reimagine him- or herself into a new story. Finally, in my own experience, this process brings to mind the way I read books or articles that are relevant to teacher research, or culture and education, issues I care about. Something written in these areas is about what I know and how I live my life. These sorts of things I read generally with great belligerence. I doubt every claim initially. And then, I would now say, I try them out imaginatively—what would this look like if it were true? I believe that these children were doing something similar.

It is necessary to take the student's unexpected behavior seriously enough to look for it in the outside world, to look for it in one's own mature encounters, in the thought of scientists or novelists or philosophers. Doing so assures that we see their behavior as a part of the tradition of human thought and action.

IDEAS FOR OTHER CHILDREN

From this experience I learned how my students' concerns with how one really knows and why one should believe the remarkable things that are written in books were resolved or worked on through unimaginative recitation, through poring over books and pictures, and through highly imaginative and argumentative participation. Further, I learned again how an inquiring attitude toward puzzling events and puzzling children established a first level of respect for them and their unfamiliar responses, a distance that kept me from taking the initiative away from them and that alerted me to their seriousness.

Then placing these various field notes and tapes together and following the threads of their thinking and mine has shown me more about the uses of the imagination and of skepticism that will be of value to other students I teach, a gift from these children to others. I see my own errors in all this, but I can't say that I regret them. They were part of the fun and feeling and occasional irritation and frustration.

CHAPTER 4

Stopping Time:
The Data of Teacher Research

The act of teaching became a daily search for the child's point of view accompanied by the sometimes unwelcome disclosure of my hidden attitudes.

—Vivian Paley, "On Listening to What Children Say"

As I have said, this book is dedicated to the idea that in order to teach more children effectively, teachers must develop their curiosity and puzzlement toward children's words and ideas, especially those words and ideas that strike us initially as less powerful and less thoughtful. The task of teacher research as I understand it is to learn about teaching and learning from the point of view of what I am calling in this book "puzzling children."

To do this, we must learn to keep records of what was said. A record "stops time"; it provides something we can look at or listen to more than once. We can share it with others and return to it another day. By stopping time, we can come to know all our students, but particularly our puzzling students, as thinkers and talkers. In this chapter I will focus on the techniques by which teacher researchers "stop time." I will discuss taping first.

TAPING

One of the most important features of taping is that it provides a full record of what was said. My recordings include what I said. When I am taking notes, I usually manage to write down a good deal of what my students say, but I generally don't have time to get my own words written down as well. Tape recordings solve this problem.

When the Brookline Teacher Research Seminar (BTRS) first began tape recording in our classrooms, one of the first things we noticed was how much we all talked and how little our students did by comparison. This was rather disturbing, and we would never have known it if we'd relied on the kinds of data that come from our memories and thoughts; journaling or field notes for example, would probably not have revealed this. The presence of the tape recorder taught us to give children more time to explain themselves. It taught us to talk less and listen more. For us this realization changed both our teaching and our research permanently (see BTRS, 2004). It was our first major research finding.

A tape can show you when children are more or less engaged because it preserves the tone of voice and the overlapping talk and other signs of excitement. Hearing children's excitement has helped me to see the direction of their thinking. You can also use the recorder to hear more children. Side conversations show up on tapes sometimes. Or when children are working in groups and you cannot be everywhere at once, you can place your tape recorder so that it will record children you're not directly speaking with.

The tape preserves for your reflection moments when children struggle to be clear or to figure something out, times when they are thinking out loud. Listen to Joshua. He was explaining what he read in a novel set in Colonial America:

JOSHUA: A lot of people going to America and there's like a packet and no children allowed.
CB: Really? No children allowed? Where does it say that?
[ ]
JOSHUA: (Reading) No child. No chil . . . chil . . . children? Child.

Joshua is convinced that the word in front of him should be "children." He keeps trying to find the word "children" so he can read "no children," but what he sees is the word "child." The book says, "No, child." He struggles to revise as he realizes that his prediction has not worked out.

Without the tape I might have only the impression that he struggled to decode. Instead, as I listened to the tape later that day, I was struck by how long he works at it and how determined he seems to be to find the word "child." I played part of the tape to colleagues and I realized as I explored it with them that Joshua had told me earlier that he thinks that children were mistreated in Colonial times because they had to work at a young age; this book, set in those times, had again shown him young children working. His prediction, that no children were allowed, was perhaps the result of his sense of indignation at the way children were treated in those days. My colleagues and I gained a vivid sense from hearing the tape of how hard he was trying to make sense of the print in a way consistent with what he found important in the book and in the history. With this in mind, I see his decoding problem in a different light. I can help him with his reading and with his sense of history and give respect to his thinking.

Many seemingly insignificant moments, for example, when a child is wrong and quickly corrected, pass almost too fast to be noticed. On my tapes I regularly hear interactions that I participated in that I have no memory of. And yet often these moments deserve further reflection.

Below is a transcript from a discussion about the water cycle that followed the "If the sun wasn't alive" conversation. We had placed cups with water in several locations in the classroom and had marked the level of the water in the cups. After a few days we were observing the level of the water in the cups and how much lower it now was.

> FRANÇOIS: It's down. The water is less. But [in a wondering tone] there's no hole in the cup [holds up cup to demonstrate that there is no hole in the bottom].
> RUBENS: The water went up.
> FABIOLA: The water went up. It evaporated up.
> FRANÇOIS: Oh . . . up.

I am fairly certain that when this conversation took place I was pleased that Rubens and Fabiola had explained the facts to François. However, I had barely noticed the conversation at all. When I heard it on the tape that evening, I had hardly any memory of it. And when I heard it on the tape I had a different reaction from that I had had in the classroom. In the quiet of my study, I could recognize that François was thinking, really wondering. We had corrected him as if it were a simple piece of information, and of course evaporation is a very familiar idea to many of us. And yet, I realized as I heard him speak, I myself only partly understand how it is that water is able to rise when almost everything else responds to gravity and falls. The idea of evaporation is one we are so used to that we are not aware that we don't really know how it works. François was thinking hard enough to realize this. Without the tape I never would have noticed his wonder. With the tape I began to wonder too. We returned to his question a few days later, and while we may not have finally explained the phenomenon, we did both honor and make progress on François's thoughts, to everyone's benefit.

These are examples of moments I would not have thought about at length if it weren't for the tape recorder. The following chapters contain many more. Of course we cannot tape everything—there would never be time to listen to the tapes.

WHEN TO TAPE

When should you turn the tape recorder or video recorder on? When are you most likely to pick up something important to think about further? I taped Joshua because he was a puzzling child. This was a one-on-one reading interview in which he was reading first silently to himself and then commenting to me on what he thought. I taped François during a science talk in a class of students who had grown accustomed to using discussion periods as times to think out loud and speak to one another. The most useful time to tape is anytime during the day when children are taking initiative, when they are thinking out loud, often when they are working with others, and when they are asking questions. These are the times when they are most likely to say something you don't expect and therefore provide you with a view into their thinking and their concerns. These are times you can especially benefit from having the opportunity to mull over their words.

When you are first trying out the practice of taping, it may be easiest to stick to small-group conversations. These have the benefit of allowing easy placement of the tape recorder or video recorder. Also, as teacher, you will have fewer management concerns with a small group and be able to allow the children to talk more spontaneously as a result. During a reading group is often a good time to tape because the conversation can be fairly free and yet the children are together in a relatively small space. Chapter 3, "Learning About Whales," contains many examples of this.

Or you might tape an interview in which you and a puzzling student talk together about something he or she is learning. Your role in this context is in many cases simply to repeat what the child said, repeat it in a questioning tone so he or she can confirm or deny that you have understood what was meant. One good question to ask is, What did you learn when we did this or that? The answers one gets to this question can be quite surprising and useful.

As you get more accustomed to the practice, it is often fruitful to leave the tape recorder on during group discussions. Make sure to listen to your tapes after any activity in which the children get excited, even chaotic, times when you are not in charge. There is often a joyful and intellectual engagement in these times that, as teachers, we cannot appreciate at the moment because we are so concerned that the children are not totally in our control. With a recording you can return to what was said to determine whether the students were on topic and who was offering ideas in this sort of context. As I have written, doing this has demonstrated to me time and time again that many puzzling children, children who in the normal classroom routine gave few clues to their thoughts, or few clues even that they were thinking, regularly engaged powerfully in these more spontaneous moments. The conversations recounted in this book are examples of this. Noticing the different participation patterns in these less controlled conversations changed our perspective on such children, and on talk in the classroom, profoundly (see Chapter 2). This was the second major research finding that resulted from taping.

LISTENING AND TRANSCRIBING

I tape many whole-class discussions and small-group conversations with students. In many cases, I like to listen to the tapes, and even transcribe parts, before I plan the next session of work. Listening to the tapes and thinking about what the children are saying is one way I do my planning. It is not really extra time—it is my planning time.

One way to get the time is to listen in the car or while doing something else. At home while cooking dinner or putting things away, I listen. It's important to have paper handy if you listen like this—there are always things you want to remember. I make notes of things to clarify for the class or for an individual child. I might transcribe a segment in which a child struggles so that I can think through what the problem is or what he or she was trying to say. I might hear a child's thought that reminds me of another thought from another day, a connection worth asking the child or the entire group about. I may find an idea or a turn of phrase that I can bring to the attention of the whole class. You don't have to listen to the entire tape to find something useful.

If you have a group you can discuss your students with, or a friend, then set a date. This is a good way to motivate yourself to listen to a transcript you will share with others. Still, there are many tapes I never get to and I hardly ever transcribe a tape fully. Tapes are a lot of trouble, but they reveal things you would not hear otherwise.

FIELD NOTES

Another way to stop the rapid flow of time in your interactions with children is to take what I call field notes. I take lots of field notes on what children say and do, and these I truly love. I write my field notes as I teach, or I write later what I can remember. I try to keep track of discussions and individual interactions, as well as activities. I take some kind of notes even if I have the tape recorder running—I can use them the next day for planning purposes, while I may not have the time to listen to the tape recording right away.

When you look at these notes later, you will find things you have no memory of, even though you yourself heard them and then thought to write them down. For me, reading field notes is at times like reading an account of a dream I had and recorded for myself during the night—I remember as I read, but I wouldn't remember very much at all if it weren't written down in front of me. This is an important thing to realize—if you are anything like me, you are teaching, making judgments and plans and interpretations from day to day on the basis of a very faulty memory. But even in a case in which you do remember, the written or scribbled record will allow you to think much further about what kids really meant or what would make sense to do next. It is important to realize that we usually operate so quickly, on such an automatic sense of what someone means or what should come next, that recognizing just the range of choices before us is often a revelation.

Also, as doing field notes becomes a habit, your memory grows. At first you sit down to write after a lively discussion and you can remember nothing. Momentarily you panic. Then, as one child's remark comes, others do too. You remember more and more. Also, the children can help you. They will usually be honored that you want to write down what they said. They will slow down during a discussion for this purpose, or wait. And they often can remember later what they meant or what they said.

There are two kinds of notes that I take—what I call "record notes" and what I call "odd moments." I will discuss them both below.

Record Notes

Taking record notes, I try to be a tape recorder. I write down what children say in my small reading groups, sometimes in large discussions, anytime they are talking. I usually try to write down everything I can once I get started, but that is never possible. When I have the time, I read these over and fill them in with other things I remember that I failed to get down at the time. Despite these efforts, they are never complete.

You may think that you will not have time to write while children are talking, but I find that writing down their ideas can be one technique for establishing a reflective tone in the discussion. The children will notice your attention. They will occasionally slow down for you. They recognize that you are taking their thoughts very seriously. I also find that for me writing during a discussion is useful in that it keeps me from talking too much. I am busy, and so the children's ideas have more space to develop. Looking over and adding to field notes later is for me a kind of meditation.

Here are some notes I took on a discussion that erupted when I was introducing Latin roots of words in different languages. I didn't expect these fifth and sixth graders to enter into a discussion on the origin of language, so I wasn't prepared to either tape or take notes at the time. I wrote these notes down later that day.

> Context: Latin discussed as source language, as reason why in Haitian Creole, French, Portuguese, and Spanish words for "carry" (*porter, pote, portar, portable*) sound similar.

> Rafael enjoyed pointing out all the letters in common between the four languages. He did it a number of times.

> Andrea suggested that there was originally one language that all the languages in the world came from.

> Theory of "telephone"—Emma suggests that languages developed like the game "telephone." That is, errors developed, and then they were maintained by some groups. She suggested that the groups would have to be far from each other or else the errors might get corrected. She said the errors could be like the errors children make when they are learning to talk.

> Jean-Pierre told the story of the Tower of Babel, the whole thing, just as though he were in Sunday school. He started by saying something like, "You want to know what happened," as if this was a special kind of true account.

> Josue and Jakil suggested it could be like a code, like hamburger might mean something to the two of them, and then someone else

misunderstands and the word has a different meaning for this person. I think I understood this.

Jakil—confusing

These notes are much sparser than some I have taken. For example, I don't have any record of what words the children actually used. But I do know whose theory was whose, something I used when we returned to this discussion. And I have a record of their energetic engagement with this question. Also, I know that I can't always understand Jakil—I will use a tape recorder next time so I can look over his words at greater length. And Rafael, repeating the letters that are the same in the four languages. He speaks both Spanish and English and he kept raising his hand and then, when I called on him, showing the letters in common between the four languages. He did it a number of times. What was he thinking?

You develop an intimacy with the children's thoughts, and a sense of wonder about their thinking, as you write down what they said and describe how they said it.

Odd Moments

Notes on odd moments are accounts of brief incidents rather than records of conversations; I am usually not writing at all when suddenly I am struck by something a child says. Then or later I write it down. Odd moments are moments when the conversation seems suddenly to step out of the expected channels of student and teacher. They can be moments of unexpected engagement, of humor, metaphor, sudden seriousness, strange connections, or a combination of these.

Diego and Humberto are discussing the scene in *The Lion, the Witch, and the Wardrobe* when Father Christmas gives out presents to the three children, each according to his or her character and needs. The boys are talking about Lucy as the kindest; that is why they say she is given the healing potion. Peter is a leader and will have to fight and so he needs the sword. Susan they say is the wisest. Diego suddenly bursts out: Who would I be in this? What would I be given and who would I be?

Diego was asking a question with great seriousness and I felt the power of his engagement. Diego said out loud something about how he is beginning to read, how he was imagining himself into books. This was not something I had heard from him in the past. He has had a very difficult family life and how this way of reading will help him as he grows I don't know, but I found it a very hopeful moment. This note helped me to know him better and it told me something about what he was learning from literature.

> Joelle and I were walking down the hall, back to the classroom, and discussing *100 Dresses*, the novel we were reading in our novel group. I said something about one of the girls who had been baiting Wanda, the main character in the book, something that indicated to Joelle, contrary to what she had thought before, that the mean girl had changed, become nicer, during the course of the novel. As we walked, Joelle suddenly burst out, "Oh, so she did change. Still I wouldn't trust those girls!" She said this with such vehemence that I was struck. She seemed to be speaking to herself, not to me.

Joelle didn't decode perfectly and often didn't comprehend accurately. I was quite concerned about her reluctance to reread when she needed to, to check back when she couldn't make sense of what she had read. Here she tentatively revised an idea she has had about the unkind girls in *100 Dresses*. She realized that perhaps they changed during the course of the story. I saw from this how she was connecting this question with her own knowledge of such girls. Still, I wouldn't trust those girls! I had not realized that the story ran counter to what she believed about mean girls—that they don't change. Nor had I realized that she was taking the question, which I had been pushing, seriously.

These field notes make little moments like these memorable, and once stuck in the mind, they often become invaluable markers or touchstones for the ongoing questions that they raise, about individuals, about how we read, and about learning.

CONNECTING TO PRACTICE

One of the key places where I do planning is in my notebook. In my notebook I write my field notes and I keep any transcript I have.

I often wander through my notebook first thing in the morning when I arrive at school, with my coffee. As I write in my notebook, I leave wide

margins and lots of empty space so that I can add more ideas, more details, and more comments. While I muse over my notebook, I add what I
call practical notes, or PNs, to what I read there. In PNs I note a next step
or a new direction for my teaching as a result of what I see written down.
I think of a question I should ask, an activity that will respond to something I've observed, a glitch that I will have to address. In the PNs is usually a good part of the planning I do each week. I often highlight them as
well so that they will stand out from other writing as I am glancing through
my notebook later. In some cases I continue writing about the same event
over a week or several weeks. In my notebook is one place where I talk to
myself, both practically and more theoretically, about children, and teaching and learning.

I include below an example of field notes that contain PNs. The PNs I
jotted down range from very specific vocabulary that seems useful to teach
in this activity, to some observations about what students are already doing
that may influence what I teach. Of course there are also many practical
ideas, and theoretical ones too, that I think about as I read my field notes
that I never manage to write down.

Writing a Play

These notes were taken during one reading period as the children
worked on writing a play and planning a performance based on a story
we had read, *The Master Thief* by the Brothers Grimm. Two students in this
group were in their final year in the Haitian bilingual program and the other
two were Haitian girls who were in the English-speaking classroom. They
were all fourth graders.

Kids trying to add dance, songs at end, ones that have nothing I can
see to do with *Master Thief.*

In practicing their intro they call the performance they will give
"Winter Festival." I have no idea where this comes from. They have
an image of this event that includes other things than I do.

PN: "Stage fright"

uses of literacy—they made lists of what they need me to get them
for the performance

Eventually as they start to act it out, they are more focused. They use the script they have written as they practice and occasionally revise

PN: "steal the wife's ring without even noticing"—Laurette's English—how to show them what this would actually mean?

Fabiola and Joelle still argue about who is old woman—is she the Master Thief in disguise or is she a new character?

PN: how do I know that the old woman is the Master Thief in disguise? Find the spot where it is clear to me and show Joelle.

IN/PN: are the children making references to the text?—*no!* not enough for me.

[Next day]

Some of their text comes out of book, or they have written it so it resembles book language—by Laurette and Hermione.

Laurette adds something about "obey"—the word "obey" strikes me as very folk talk like. Is it from the text?

Hermione wrote an ending, but it seems that she did it without much engagement

Hermione says she wants no violence in this play.

COMMENTS ON THE FIELD NOTES

In my field notes at the top I noted that the kids kept referring to a dance in the play. Evidently they thought there should be a dance in this play, although I couldn't imagine why—there is certainly no dance in the Grimm story.

In practicing their welcome to the audience too, I noted that they often call the performance a "Winter Festival." I wrote these things down because I was totally surprised. I had no idea at the time where they came from. As I wrote in my notes, the children seemed to have an image of this play that contained other things than what my image contained.

Because I had written it down, and because I discussed it with others, since it seemed funny, I had the opportunity to go over this idea of the dance a number of times. It was while I was doing this that I realized that dances are regularly a part of Haitian folk tales, and that perhaps my students, familiar with this tradition, were feeling the lack, and wondering if they might need to add one.

I noted the phrase "stage fright" because I found that they did not know this term. They told me they feared that they would be embarrassed when we performed. I wanted to remember to use "stage fright" a number of times so they could learn it. So this was a very practical note.

I noted the lists they spontaneously made of props, mainly things they wanted me to collect for them. I was wondering about their recognition of the need to make lists. Their parents in Haiti, from what I knew of them, rarely made lists, since paper and pencil, as well as reading and writing skills, were scarce in many cases. I have often found Haitian children not taking naturally to the American view of list making, but in this case they were ahead of me. Perhaps this was cross-cultural communication—they knew I needed lists and this one was for me. Or was this field note bringing to my attention a context in which we both felt we needed lists? In the past I had noticed only when we disagreed on the need for a list, but here was a context in which we agreed.

Because I note things, I am able to recognize them as they change and develop. They don't slide by me invisibly. I think I dismissed the dance idea when it first came up, but because the children stuck to it, and because I had written it down, I was able to reflect on it a bit more, and I decided to watch and see what happened without my intervening. Lists and where they are necessary might become an important teaching point or might not, I didn't know, but it seemed worth noting.

I also noted when they used the text of the folk tale as a source for their play, and when they seemed to have re-created a sense of the folk tale language in what they wrote. "Obey" was an example of what I felt was literary language appropriate to this fairy tale. I have to make decisions about when to teach something, and when to let them figure things out for themselves, and these kinds of notes help me to see what students are already doing and what I can build on.

Joelle, who spoke with great informality and fluency in English, had missed a point in the plot where the reader is expected to recognize that the Master Thief is disguising himself. Hearing the girls argue about this made first me and then Joelle more aware of the problem she was having and the close reading that the story required. Eventually we changed the plot slightly to allow for a character to be pushed, rather than shot, in deference to Hermione's wish for no violence.

CONCLUSION

In many cases the notes I make and moments on tape that I notice and find most useful to my thinking begin because I am surprised. The idea of a dance where one hadn't existed, Diego's outburst in *The Lion, The Witch, and the Wardrobe*, Rafael commenting on the same letters in related words a number of times, François noticing that there were no holes in the cup from which water had disappeared, all surprised and puzzled me and eventually caused me to think further about the subject matter I was teaching as well as the children's approaches to it. But very likely I would have forgotten the incidents, or would not have remembered them so well, if I had not had a record. Keeping them in mind, reflecting further and writing down more thoughts, discussing them with others, re-experiencing these moments, all brought me a sense of intimacy with the thinking of these children that I valued for itself, and that I could also use as I taught them.

The ultimate goal of teacher research is to see deeply into the true possibilities of our students and to find significant forms of engagement between them and what we are teaching. Their preoccupations, their mistakes, their odd remarks help us to see the things we are teaching in new and interesting light, often deepening our understanding. This is an inquiry that never ends. The techniques we use must help to keep us open to new answers, new responses at all times. Stopping time supports a continuing process of following our puzzlement, our curiosity, and our uncertainty.

CHAPTER 5

Who Gets to Feel Scientific?

Initially in any class there are some children whose ideas just stun us because they seem so powerful. Wow, we may think, let everyone hear that. And there are others who seem to be on a different planet. It is a very common complaint of teachers that we can't teach to such a range. In this chapter I want to explore this issue. Is this range a problem or a resource? Is it a range in ability or instead a diversity in approach? Can very different children learn from each other?

This chapter contains an account of a discussion that has many of the features I have been discussing: Much of the control was with the children. They were discussing a common experience. The question was their own. It has been one major argument of this book that such a discussion provides a context in which the children who generally seem to have fewer academic advantages, the puzzling children, reveal themselves as thinkers, sometimes in surprising ways. In this chapter I will focus in particular on children learning from one another.

THE CLASSROOM AND CHILDREN

In the two-way Spanish bilingual classroom I describe in this chapter there were children from many backgrounds. For some of them, Spanish was their first language; for others, English was. Many of these children were highly successful in school, and, of course, there were also some who were not. We will be looking at two children in particular, Serena and Elena.

Let me first introduce this classroom. This was Marcia Pertuz's third-grade classroom. Pertuz organizes her curriculum around tasks that are real and demanding in many different ways, from writing poetry to doing science. She is interested above all in creating independent learners. As she says, "I strive to put my children in charge of their own learning, set up situations in which they have to problem-solve, and stay out of their way while they think." Pertuz was a member of the CKC Seminar. Pertuz had been reading Karen Gallas's book *Talking Their Way into Science* (1995). Gallas emphasizes using the children's own questions to pursue scientific study and she emphasizes as well giving the children a large amount of control in the conversations. Pertuz decided to try these policies out in her science instruction. As a member of the CKC staff, I was helping Pertuz to explore these science talks as she tried them out. We videotaped the talks. We met regularly to look at the tapes and discuss them with another teacher from the bilingual program and other members of CKC staff.

Now to our two focal children, Serena and Elena. Serena was very much at home in both Spanish and English, and in academic language in both. She was the child of university professors, one from Colombia and the other from the United States; she was considered an excellent student. Serena's strengths were in many ways familiar to most educators.

Elena's mother was an immigrant from Mexico who worked in restaurants. Her father was rarely around. Elena spoke both Spanish and English at home. She did not strike the average listener as a sophisticated learner. Elena was not seen as a strong student. In fact, she had not been promoted at the end of the previous year.

Could Elena possess intellectual strengths that would help Serena and her other classmates? These were two very different students. However, in this conversation, I believe that Elena's approach was found the more useful by her classmates. Her ways of considering the topic both changed the students' participation patterns to include more children and also led to an unusual probing and wondering that clarified and deepened their understanding of what they were discussing.

The children in Pertuz's classroom had been growing Wisconsin Fast Plants. These are a genetically engineered variety of the mustard plant that is particularly useful for some classroom studies because the plants move through the cycle from seed to flower to seed again in only 45 days. The children had begun by planting their seeds and measuring the plants as they began to grow. Pertuz had been collecting the children's questions about plants as they did this and posting them on the wall. Once a week she asked one child from the classroom to choose a question from the list for the class to discuss in science talk. On this day the question Do plants grow every day? was chosen.

I will include here a large part of the conversation the children had on this question, alternating the children's words in normal print with my thoughts in italics. I will be attempting to identify the scientific and mathematical ideas that the children were developing and also to explore the ways in which Elena in particular proposed her ideas on these topics. I will also be contrasting Elena's approach with Serena's. While I don't mean to stereotype either child on the basis of one conversation, Serena's response in this conversation represents for me a response closer to the goals many educators would have for such a conversation, a response whose power is easily visible. While most teachers would also honor Elena's participation and recognize that she is thinking hard, the power of her approach as scientific and mathematical thought is less easy for many of us to see. I hope to show the intellectual power in Elena's approach and to demonstrate how it deepened the questions and the understanding of all the students.

THE TALK: TRANSCRIPT AND ANALYSIS

Serena immediately responds to the discussion question, Do plants grow everyday?: "It's so obvious. They grow all the time and so do we. . . . Our eyes can't see it."

But Carlita asks her: "If you can't see it, how can you tell it's happening?"

Serena seems to be saying that "seeing" growth like you see someone walking is not possible, it goes on so slowly, in such tiny increments. But Carlita asks her how she knows then, that it's happening at all.

Serena responds to her, "Don't you grow every day? [Carlita nods.] Then these ones do."

Another child disagrees: "We don't grow every day," she says. Lara chimes in with her ideas on the subject: "On our birthday. On our birthday, we grow."

Then the following exchange takes place:

SERENA: When you finally notice that someone's grown they just grow like that?" [Serena moves her hands apart suddenly to demonstrate fast growth.]
LARA: Only one day they grow that fast?
ELENA: I only grow in months. That's—

SERENA: Do you see yourself growing? All of a sudden at midnight you grow like this [moves hands apart a few inches quickly] and then the next day at night you grow like this [same gesture].

Lara talks about growing only on her birthday—perhaps she is thinking of when one's age changes. At another point in the conversation, she mentions that she has a growth chart for her height at home—perhaps she is measured always on her birthday. Elena, too, when she talks about only growing in months, may be thinking about the way we talk about age; we might say someone is 2 years 9 months, or 6 months old, but we rarely calibrate age to the day. Rather we talk about age in years and months. Or maybe Elena is thinking about the amount of time that must pass before one is aware that one has grown—you don't notice it on a day-to-day basis. Serena seems to be reminding them of her idea that all the growing must take place over time, not all at once, even if it appears so. Her offering, "all of a sudden at midnight," seems to take the most extreme case to show the absurdity of growing all at once, rather than steadily. Serena is arguing logically, but also in a rhetorically playful way. One wonders how the children respond to this idea of growing at the exotic hour of "midnight."

A little later Elena enters the conversation with an account of her experience watching her plant.

I think it does grow every day because every single day—every single day we look at the plant. . . . Every single day we look at the plants and it's growing a little bit more. Then we look again and then it—and then tomorrow we look again and it's—it's growing a little bit more. And the other—to—today—yes—I mean—I think it was Wednesday that—n- no [pause] today's Wednesday [pause] it was Tuesday that I looked at my plant and it was all crooked and it's getting—it's getting stronger and the little piece, the little piece that they have on there—I had a little teeny, teeny, teeny one—now it's fat.

The first thing of note here is that what Elena says here is much more than she usually has to say on any topic in school. What does she choose to say in this long utterance, so uncharacteristic of her? Elena has stayed very close to her experience of observing the plant itself. She seems to be seeing it again in her mind and noticing things even as she gives her account. As she recalls her memory of the way the plant has changed, she includes as an example of growth the development of what she calls the "little pieces," which are in fact the seedpods, and she mentions as well the development of greater strength. The children have been charting the height of their plants, measuring from the soil to the highest point. They have been considering height and growth largely as one and the same. Elena here offers some new ideas on what might count as growth, namely, getting fat, getting stronger.

As Elena goes on to describe what she has seen, she also begins exploring ideas about the rate of growth. At first, as she says, "every single day we look at the plants and it's growing a little bit more. Then we look again and then it—and then tomorrow we look again and it's—it's growing a little bit more"—here she is describing her sense of steady, gradual growth—every day a little bit more. In contrast, her final comment, emphasized by the way she uses her intonation, suggests a jump in growth, a growth spurt. She says, "The little piece that they have on there—I had a little teeny, teeny, teeny one—now it's fat." She emphasizes "teeny, teeny, teeny," using a high, steady, emphatic pitch and repeating the word three times. The repetition and the steady rhythm of "teeny, teeny, teeny" suggests how long it was the same. Then she speeds up her speech and lowers her pitch for "now it's fat." Using rhythm this way emphasizes, and almost enacts, the sudden contrast between when it was teeny, and "now." One could almost understand her meaning without words—with only the pitch and rhythm.

Changes in rhythmic pattern and pitch like this are often part of the surprise endings used in stories told in social situations to amuse others; here the change has additional relevance in that the two rhythms represent rather directly the two kinds of growth that are under discussion; slow and steady is one rate of growth, sudden and rapid being another. A narrative strategy, something in which probably all the children have practice and skill, has been brought into the service of a scientific and mathematical distinction relevant to their developing question on growth and measurement.

However, the discussion now moves to a different approach to seeing growth as Pertuz, the teacher, asks, "But does anybody notice when they looked at their plant some days there was no growth at all?" Serena nods and replies to Pertuz:

SERENA: Our rulers can't be perfect.

*Although she asks whether anyone looked at their plant and saw no
growth, Pertuz is probably thinking of the growth charts the children have
been keeping as the place where growth or no growth might be seen.
Pertuz goes on to ask how many times the children saw this "no growth,"
which seems again to be a reference to the measurements taken for their
charts. Serena certainly takes it this way, as she answers from her knowledge of the chart she has been keeping and the measurements that it
records. She questions whether or not their rulers can always "detect"
growth and thus whether or not the growth charts reliably indicate by the
numbers charted whether or not the plant has grown. Serena and her
teacher are "seeing" growth through these numbers recorded on paper,
although with some critical awareness of the limitations of the tool. Elena,
on the other hand, seems to look at the plant for her evidence. This is a
very normal moment in a conversation, where people are talking about the
same thing, but not exactly. Without the transcript to peruse, it is unlikely
that any of us would have noted the difference here in what various people
are looking at. This distinction in how different participants "see" growth
is a theme I will follow in the rest of this discussion.*

Susannah and Serena next collaborate to suggest that it is easier to see
the growth of the plants over the weekend, when "we're not there."

SUSANNAH: Serena is right because every day when—when we're
    like—every week we get bigger and bigger.
SERENA: But we can't tell.
SUSANNAH: But we can't tell. We just get one inch bigger.
SERENA: Until—
SUSANNAH: And then weeks—on weekends when we're not here
    they get bigger too.
PERTUZ: So you've noticed a big difference over—from Friday to
    Monday?
SUSANNAH: Yeah, they were like this little. Every week we get
    bigger and bigger.
SERENA: But we can't tell.
SUSANNAH: But we can't tell. We just get one inch bigger.
[Lots of cross talk among students.]
SERENA: If we were ever 28 years old what would tell that we have
    grown? What would tell? Unless you have a grow chart and
    you grow yourself like every year you'll see that—

LARA: I do. I mark myself on the wall. I would say I'm more bigger.
SERENA: And then—
SUSANNAH: In the week, when we came back Monday my plant was
    a little bit big. Every week we grow bigger but we can't tell.

*This piece of the conversation is largely co-constructed by Susannah and
Serena. Like Elena, Susannah is a student who has difficulty in many
school situations, a student who is not at home in academic language in
English or Spanish and rarely has much to say in class. In a sort of
rhythm with Serena's prompts—"until," "but we can't tell"—Susannah
here argues that over time small changes may become visible. She focuses
not on the ruler, as Serena did earlier, but on the plant itself, and on
herself, in relation to the time between views. If we don't look at our plants
every day, if we wait over a weekend before we look again, we may be able
to see that there has been growth. It is possible that Serena's "but we can't
tell" is referring to a way of "telling" different from Susannah's, one
relying on measurement tools and their imperfections. It seems probable
that Susannah is talking about differences one could see by looking
directly at the plant, or at oneself.*

Juana seems to be responding to the "but we can't tell" as she asks in
a tone of deep concern:

JUANA: How come we can't really see it—us grow and the plants—
    how come we can't see the plants grow and how come we can't
    see us grow?
SERENA: Well, if we had a chart for them—

*Serena answers Juana, again from her experience of using the chart—"if
we had a chart for them." But Juana seems to want to see growth by
looking directly at the plant and to see it as it happens, "really see" it. She
appears not so taken with the power of the numbers and the growth chart
to demonstrate growth.*

Elena next attempts to answer Juana:

I think I got the answer to Juana's question. That I don't—I don't
think we could see them grow but I think they could feel theirselves
grow. Sometimes we can feel ourselves grow because my feet grow

so fast cuz this little crinkly thing is always bothering my feet. That means it's starting to grow. It's starting to stretch out.

Elena, like Juana, seems to be thinking about growth in its minute-to-minute aspect. How would the plant feel? she wonders, and how would she feel? She uses her body to explore this. She wriggles her nose as she describes the crinkles in her feet, and she makes her voice high and throaty as if to feel the air as she speaks. It seems she is trying to experience again, and at the same time dramatize for others, the crinkly feeling of growth. She is speaking from a perspective inside her body as it grows, rather than observing from outside.

A few turns later, Juana herself responds:

I have two things to say. How—what makes the plants grow so slow? . . . and I think I can kinda see myself grow because one day I putted on my socks and they was too small for me so I can fit in my mom's socks now.

Recall that a little earlier Juana was asking how one could know something had grown, if one couldn't see it happen. She is now relying on a measurement system of sorts to answer this concern; it is not the usual measurement system, but a measurement system that has features that evidently satisfy her. It seems that she could feel when she put on her old socks that they were too small. Perhaps it was a "crinkly feeling." Juana seems to be combining Elena's way of feeling growth with a measurement system over time, as suggested in different ways by Serena and Susannah—her feet don't fit, then her feet do fit. Wearing her mom's socks allows her to, as she says, "see [herself] grow."

Susannah continues in a similar fashion as she remembers the change in clothing size that her little brother has gone through—he was a size 5 when he was little; now he's a 10. She speeds up as she says, "Now he's a 10," echoing Elena's way of representing the growth of the seedpods and similarly suggesting that the change was sudden and remarkable.

At the end of this discussion we find the children seeking to understand the role of the sun in plant growth. They say that they have been told that the sun helps plants to grow, but, they ask, how? A number of the children have their arms outstretched as if they were branches and leaves, as they ask, How does the sun get inside and what does it do? Serena too insists, "But how?" trying to imagine along with the others what this process could be like. As they explore their questions about the role of the sun, there is a good deal of laughter and cross talk. They turn toward each other. They seem thrilled with the difficulty of their question. They are clearly deeply engaged, asking for more information, trying to imagine the process by which the sun gets inside the plant to do whatever it does. This is a level of questioning you rarely get from children of any age, a sense of evaluating an answer as insufficient, a desire to see beyond an easy explanation. Here we have a level playing field with all the children wondering, those who "knew" about photosynthesis and those who had not heard of it before.

STUDENTS' LEARNING

What have the children learned here? First of all, they have explored different kinds of growth. Serena refers to the charts they have made that kept track of height. Other children recall their observations, imagine the plant, remember feelings, tell stories in which they represent in various ways the changes that they have noted in plants and in people. Susannah talks of the change in her little brother's size. Lara mentions the growth chart she has at home and her birthday, Juana her sock size. These are not just example upon example. Rather, with the help of the tape recorder and transcript, we can see that linear measurement as a system for noting growth has been reorganized into only one part of a set of ideas; the children are now seeing that growth includes ideas of volume, constant versus intermittent rates of growth, as well as the development of important new parts (seedpods). And that there are many ways to notice growth.

Furthermore, these different aspects of growth involve taking different perspectives on the phenomenon as well. Serena measured her plant and then spoke of growth from the numbers she recorded and her understanding of how rulers work. She did not talk about the plant itself. In contrast, Elena and a number of other students looked at the "grower" itself. Seeing, or even feeling growth in this way led all the children to wonder about the process of growth, rather than just the visible result.

Based on experience with many similar conversations, I believe that Elena's way of participating was crucial in inviting others into this conversation and in making it a powerful space for thinking. What Elena was able to do in this conversation is a skill that I regularly see in children from bilingual and minority homes, children of less educated parents. And yet it is not one that we regularly honor or even make room for in classrooms. What did she do? First, she returned the discussion to the plant, although perhaps not the plant as physically present but the plant as she remembered it and as she imagined it. And she brought imagined and remembered experiences of her own growth into the conversation. Elena employs her imagination and memory to "see" growth. She tells two little stories, one based in close observation of the plant and her memory of that, and one in her sensory memory of her own growth. She uses her voice to demonstrate a sense of growth itself, and the different rates by which it might proceed. Her voice mimics the rapid growth of the pods. She appears to be trying to be "growth," rather than to be an outsider observing it. She explores what growth might feel like inside, crinkling her nose and recalling her "crinkly feet." She brings drama and impersonation into the conversation.

Elena makes use of her intimate relation with growth and with her plant. She takes seriously what she already knows of growth, what she has experienced, and seeks to know new things in the same way—as a thinker and also a participant. Is this a scientific way of thinking? It brings to mind the way the Nobel Prize–winning biologist Barbara McClintock spoke of her work with corn genes:

> I start with the seedling, and I don't want to leave it. I don't feel I really know the story if I don't watch the plant all the way along. So I know every plant in the field. I know them intimately, and I find it a great pleasure to know them.
>
> When I was really working with them I wasn't outside, I was down there. I was part of the system. I was right down there with them, and everything got big. I even was able to see the internal parts of the chromosomes—actually everything was there. It surprised me because I actually felt as if I was right down there and these were my friends. As you look at these things, they become part of you. And you forget yourself. (quoted in Fox-Keller, 1983, p. 165)

Elena has chosen an approach that is similar in some ways. She is trying to be a fellow creature with the plants, to feel their growing life as she feels her own. Like McClintock, she doesn't want to leave the plants behind for the numbers about them. Serena makes a logical connection between human growth and plant growth—"don't you grow every day? Then these ones do"—while Elena's connection is different, organized around shared experience. She tries to see, or feel, growth from within.

Her doing this seems to have prompted other children to reconsider experiences of their own in light of this topic. The topic expanded to include their ways of connecting to it. Susannah's knowledge of her brother's clothing size and Juana's change of socks are probably not experiences that, when they happened, struck the child as being on the topic of growth or as relevant to the question of whether or not we, or plants, grow every day; rather these experiences were re-seen through this conversation.

The kind of thinking Elena modeled here represents a world she created and invited the others into, a world in which their own already powerful ways of thinking can function. The children here are excited to discover the importance of their own experience. And, as a result, they are committed to the idea that explanations need to make sense to them and that their own ideas are sensible. They ask serious questions. If you can't see growth, why can't you?—this is not a question one usually thinks to ask. They challenge someone to explain to them how photosynthesis works, rather than just accepting that that is something that happens. In the context of this discussion, then, it is more possible for the children to question knowledge that they would have taken for granted. They try to get inside the phenomenon in various ways based on their experience. They go beyond what the teacher and the curriculum expect into deeper and more complex views and concerns.

I am certainly not arguing that what Serena knows is not also valid. Moving from the organism to the data collected about that organism is surely one of the ways science is able to progress. It makes all kind of comparisons and analyses possible. But it is also true, as the Barbara McClintock example demonstrates, that an intimate and imaginative connection with the life of the phenomenon under study is part of the process of science. Elena has been crucial in introducing this approach to knowing to her classmates. She has added to the definition of growth, presenting it from the inside and as including a range of developments, and she has promoted her recognition that what we already know about growth connects with this new knowledge and new situation.

This conversation, and many of the others explored in this book, demonstrate, I believe, that when one shifts the kind of talk encouraged in classroom discussion, a different pattern of talent and achievement emerge. Children from all backgrounds have been thinking and have their own ways to approach new tasks and new understandings. The children have a good deal to learn from each other.

CHAPTER 6

Making the Familiar Strange

Many of us initially look at a chunk of transcript or a set of field notes and feel overwhelmed: How should we begin? It can be hard to see anything extraordinary or thought-provoking in the words and activity of children we already know well, as they talk and act in curriculum we have perhaps done many times. What can possibly be contained in all the words we have collected that would show us the child in a new light? How can we develop enough distance from this familiar material to challenge our understanding of teaching and learning?

Below I describe some practices that I have found useful in exploring the transcripts and notes I collect. First, for those of my readers who have the support of a teachers' group, I suggest some ways that the group conversation might be organized to promote reflective and thoughtful response. Second, I offer some strategies that have helped me notice useful ideas in children's words.

TEACHERS' GROUPS

Sharing the children's ideas and words with others is a crucial way to begin to see them in a new light. When I tell a story from the classroom to other people they often respond in unexpected ways—they understand something I didn't, they are reminded of something else, they laugh or worry when I wouldn't—and in doing so, they help me to gain distance from my own automatic response, my assumptions. They show me more possibilities. The teachers I cite in "If the sun was not alive" who mentioned their own feelings about the moon and its protective, almost mothering qualities are an example of this.

And yet teachers tend to give one another advice. This may or may not be welcome. Teachers are often oriented toward practical solutions to problems. We don't always take the time to explore a problem before we suggest answers or solutions. We also are prone to make interpretations based on ideas we already have or beliefs about particular children that we cannot prove. Perhaps everyone does, but teacher research requires that we take children's ideas seriously, examine the details, and even question our preexisting ideas. The following are two examples of protocols developed to help groups do this.

Taking Roles: Chèche Konnen

The Chèche Konnen Center (CKC) was founded as a seminar for K–8 teachers in urban classrooms who wished to improve their teaching of science (for a fuller description, see Rosebery & Warren, 1998). Most teachers' commitment was for a minimum of 3 years, usually more. During that time teachers would attend a meeting approximately once a month. While I was involved the meetings typically included two parts: ongoing work on a long-term science investigation conducted by teachers and sharing data (transcripts, videotapes, student work) from classrooms. Thus we learned science together and explored the ideas the children had; these children were sometimes studying the same areas of science, sometimes different areas.

For the data share, CKC teachers would take turns choosing, with staff help or independently, a piece of data, usually a few minutes of videotape, from their classrooms. The data might be chosen as a way to bring a concern or a question to the group or the data might simply be an example of the children in an exciting discussion. A transcript would be made.

Each participant would be assigned a child to focus on. If there was a video we would watch it first and each of us would listen especially for the child we had been assigned. The group would then read the transcript out loud together, each of us speaking the role of our focal child. The discussion would begin with participants trying to describe the ideas and point of view of the child whose part they had read. Others were allowed to jump in as the discussion continued, but we always began by each of us taking responsibility for uncovering the ideas of our own particular child.

This system functioned well to focus participants on the children's words and on the transcript. It kept us grounded in the data. It was also a way to make sure that even students who said little received a fair share of attention.

In focusing on the children's words, the spotlight was off the teacher. The discussion was less about his or her lesson and more about how the children were thinking and talking; insights into their talk and ideas affected how the teacher would hear them in the future and in this way addressed issues of practice nevertheless. Of course it often happened that once we came to an understanding of the children's ideas, we all could see that the teacher had not understood them at the time—but this was expected and normal and usually just made us laugh at ourselves. We came to very much agree with Vivian Paley (1986) when she said, "The range of possibilities for misunderstandings is quite astonishing. And is this not a lucky circumstance? It means we ought never to run out of great curriculum materials, free for the asking."

In addition, because we learned science together in CKC, we had recent experience with the great variety of ways to engage with new ideas. We were able to recognize new value in forms of the children's engagement, such as stories, use of metaphor, the acting out of ideas; learning science together in CKC, we saw that we too used stories and metaphor and drama in our learning.

Whittier Inquiry Group: Protocols for Group Talk

The following approach to establishing a reflective space comes from the Whittier Inquiry Group. This is a group of K–6 teachers who teach in Chicago in a largely Mexican American school. In their meetings teachers take turns presenting a child they are concerned about or sometimes a conversation from their classroom. The problem they address with this protocol is the habit that participants sometimes have of jumping to conclusions and making inferences before they have carefully observed. They were influenced in developing this protocol by the work of Patricia Carini (e.g., Carini, 1979). Below is their description of what they do.

1. Getting started: The group chooses a facilitator to guide participants through each phase of the meeting. The presenting teacher shares the student data (student work, video recording, transcription, field notes) without making comments. Teachers may also choose to describe a puzzling event or share a burning question.
2. Describing the data: Participants, one by one, identify any aspect of the data they may notice. They don't make judgments about the quality of the work; they don't try to explain why it is the way it is or share their personal preferences. The goal is to share objective

observations. There may be multiple rounds of sharing observations. The presenting teacher writes the observations down.

3. Raising questions: In this step, participants may ask questions to help clarify the teacher's goals, the task, or other considerations.

4. Reflections and wonderments: In this step participants attempt to see the world through the student's eyes on the basis of the observations the group has made. The goal is to share ideas about what the evidence suggests that the child is thinking or feeling, his or her intentions and ways of expressing himself. The term *wonderment* is used to indicate that these ideas are often very speculative—we can't be sure.

5. The presenting teacher shares: The presenting teacher is invited to share any thoughts or new questions that have been stimulated by this examination of student work.

6. Implications for teaching and learning: Participants share the ideas and questions for their own practice that have been stimulated by this discussion.

The Whittier group has been together for quite a few years now and the members tell me that they no longer always strictly follow this protocol. They believe that it has been very useful to them in establishing the difference between judgments and inferences, on the one hand, and a reflective response tied to the data, on the other. They return to it on occasion, especially when there are new members present.

Both these protocols have the effect of distancing the teacher from his or her first impressions of the child and the child's words. Hearing other points of view seems to loosen the glue of our assumptions, so that we can think about whether or not they are correct.

GETTING INTO THE DATA

Data is what I call the words from the classroom that I have been able to collect. I call it *data* because it is what I will interpret. The following are a few strategies that have been helpful to me when I am poring over transcripts and field notes of the things students say.

Restating each child's ideas in my own words often gets me started. But I find also, as I have said, that the more I share what the child said with others, the better I understand. I also on occasion ask the child again. The children can often tell you a lot, even quite a while later.

Second, I look through the transcript to see how ideas are being presented. Are ideas coming from jokes or exaggeration? Are they coming from stories about events that took place elsewhere? Doing this helps me to understand what connections they are making. It also provides me with a surer sense of what words and experiences to reference as we continue our work together.

Third, I particularly focus on what puzzles me. I look for anything that surprises. I want to know how we are different. Like many teachers, I learn a great deal about what I am teaching by exploring the unexpected things that children notice. I want to know what they think is important that I do not. Further, I want to know more about their wrong answers and what they must be thinking to be wrong in that way. When I ask children what they have learned after a particular day, I am often astonished by what they think of to say.

When you are beginning to do this work, you might just take a piece of instruction, a lesson, a discussion, and focus on everything in your notes or tapes that you found less valuable. Then try to figure out what was going on in those contributions and how you would build on them. Was there anything relevant to the topic of instruction that you had missed? This is something I still have to make myself do—I never get over missing the point in the ideas of some kids.

TAKING IT SERIOUSLY

Having determined as well as I can what the children meant and how they explained themselves, I then ask myself, and my colleagues, to consider this talk in relation to other mature forms: How is this talk and activity similar to or different from what would count as a literate or academic understanding of the material? Have the students noticed something or done something that a professional writer, scientist, historian, and so on, would? Or are there situations outside school in which their ideas would be considered adult and appropriate? When I am fortunate enough to know a professional in the field I am teaching—a writer, if I am discussing a novel, or a botanist or a geologist, if we are working in that area, I may send him or her thoughts from the students to see if I can get any different insight. I sent some of the thoughts of Herve and his classmates about whales to a friend who is a biologist, and I managed to locate a Brazilian botanist, a friend of our kindergarten teacher, who responded to a number of the ideas about erosion that are discussed in Chapter 9. Sometimes just an interested person will offer important understandings. Book group members, for example, are often eager to think about how and why we read literature. These sources help you to see the serious intentions in children's work that you might otherwise miss.

The ideas and words of children surround teachers like noisy air. Making what seems so familiar and so transitory into something still, something strange, worthy of rephrasing, comparison, of exchanging with others, is a form of meditation, I think. It is another way to know children and to learn as a teacher.

CHAPTER 7

"Vloop Vloop":
Children Talk About Metamorphosis

In this chapter I present a conversation in which children were out of their seats, joking and occasionally arguing and interrupting and generally making their points with exceptional drama and humor. As teachers, we may appreciate the scene, but it also often makes us nervous. I explore the question I had and so many of us ask when we observe children engaging in such animated and informal discussion in school: Are they just having fun? Are they learning the things they need to know, the vocabulary words, facts and concepts? What *are* they learning exactly? In this chapter I address these questions in particular, with reference to a fifth grader named Jean-Charles as he studies insect metamorphosis.

Jean-Charles was a fairly solemn child, not a storyteller or a joker like many of his classmates. It frequently took him a long time to begin to speak, and the class often had to wait while he formulated his thoughts. He was considered to have difficulty organizing language both in English and in Haitian Creole, and he had been referred to special education for this problem. Jean-Charles was a puzzling child. Students like Jean-Charles often seem to have enormous gaps in their knowledge. They don't appear to speak precisely or even "correctly." Jean-Charles, in fact, had a great deal to teach me. We will consider his learning in discussion and then later in an interview.

I was not the teacher in the classroom I will describe here. I include this chapter because I learned a huge amount about talk and learning from my participation in that class. As a CKC staff member I spent considerable time over 2 years visiting and documenting the bilingual class of Sylvio Hyppolite and Pat Berkley. Theirs was a classroom of Haitian students from the fifth through the eighth grade. It was a transitional bilingual classroom; the children were expected to move into the mainstream classrooms in 3 years. Pat was in charge of the older students and Sylvio the younger, but the whole group did science together. I attended their periods of science instruction and videotaped these teachers and their students as they studied science as part of the work of the CKC seminar. I took notes on what they and their students said and then showed them to Pat and Sylvio as part of CKC's joint process of planning next steps.

EXPANDING THE TALK

Let me first introduce the teachers and their goals with regard to talk. During this particular year, Sylvio, who had grown up in Haiti, had developed a commitment to exploring the value of his students' everyday ways of talking in constructing scientific knowledge. This had been prompted by an experience in the CKC seminar.

In the seminar we often looked at videotapes from participants' classrooms. One discussion we looked at featured a class of Haitian bilingual students studying snails (see Warren & Rosebery, 1996). One student had taken home a jar of snails over a long weekend, snails that the students had collected as part of a pond study. When the student returned with the snails after 3 days, he claimed that he had three generations of snails. The other students did not believe him and challenged him aggressively. The tape captured for us this argument and the way the students were laughing and posturing as they argued.

The Haitian members of the seminar told the rest of us that the way the children were joking as they argued reminded them of how Haitian people often talk in social situations, taking pleasure in the skill of challenge and response. It also reminded them of the loud, usually cheerful wrangling that their own students engaged in over soccer games and other playground activities. As we watched the videotape more than once, however, we were also able to confirm our impression that, jokes notwithstanding, these students were staying on the topic of snail reproduction and constructing a good critique of the first student's methodology—what he should have done in the way he organized his snails for his claim to be more convincing.

Haitian students are usually thought of as rather quiet in science class. Since they generally come from religious families, and also often from ones in which the parents were able to get relatively little education, many people have assumed that Haitian students know little about science in general and still less about the uses of evidence and logical argumentation in science. And yet it became clear from exploring the transcript that these children were well able to participate in a classroom culture based on evidence, experimentation, and precise definitions. To this point, Sylvio's students had been very quiet and respectful as well. Sylvio became committed to admitting this other kind of talk into his classroom.

Pat had not been a good science student in school. Her experience of learning science in the CKC seminar had opened up for her the possibility that her way of thinking about the world, which in her education she had been led to believe was utterly unscientific, might have more value in developing scientific explanation than she had thought (Berkley, 1994). As a result, she was enormously patient with students as they tried to explain themselves, and she became very reluctant to regard any idea that a student presented as not relevant or useful. Thus both Pat and Sylvio, each from his or her own perspective, had become committed to expanding their classroom expectations to include the students' everyday talk and reasoning for the following year.

As a way of enacting this commitment, Pat and Sylvio decided to institute what they called "science circle" as a part of their curriculum in science. Science circles, as they developed, became group conversations in which the children came together to form a circle so everyone could see one another; these usually occurred a few times a week. These talks were places to explore questions that had come up, to share observations and results from the students' science work and to discuss readings.

The talks might begin in English, depending on who was leading that day, but as the children became engaged they would often talk a good deal in Haitian Creole (HC), the language the children knew best. On many occasions children would switch back and forth between HC and English as they spoke. Pat, who did not speak very much HC, did not stop the children when they carried on conversations she could not understand. As an English as a second language teacher, she was very concerned to provide opportunities for them to improve their English, but she had also come to have enormous faith in the children's seriousness and reasoning, even when she could not follow this reasoning herself. In science she felt they should speak in whatever language they chose. She would simply ask for a translation after a time.

A TALK ON METAMORPHOSIS

To present what the children learned through these sometimes rollicking conversations, I will explore a transcript from a science circle and then follow Jean-Charles's understanding through his participation in this talk and in a later interview on the same subject. The discussion took place after the class had spent some weeks watching mealworms move through stages of metamorphosis. Each team of students had a petri dish of a few mealworms and they had been keeping track of the number of skin changes, measuring how big the mealworm was at the time and when the change took place. This day they were working their way through a written text, in English, on metamorphosis. The students were taking turns reading the English aloud, then discussing what they had read paragraph by paragraph in Creole. Manuelle, after reading what a great deal the larvae eat before they turn into pupae, asked, apparently humorously, "Why, if people eat and eat they don't change their skin, they don't transform, the way insects do?" Sylvio, the teacher, asked the students to comment on Manuelle's question. The book was put away and a science talk ensued.

After Manuelle asks why people don't change, if they eat a huge amount, one child reminds her that our skin does peel.

Manuelle returns, "But we don't transform."

Fabiola says, "God did not create us like insects"; she evidently means that that's why we don't transform.

Rudolphe brings in basketball: "If you play basketball, you get dirty, when you bathe, your skin comes off with the dirt." He is suggesting that we do, in fact, like the larvae, change our skin.

Marianne responds to this claim, "It's not all people who do that." She gets up to demonstrate how slowly some people walk, implying they don't play hard and get all dirty and then change some of their skin while bathing.

Junior says that he has learned on television that your skin rubs off inside your clothes.

Stefan, a new student, makes a general statement: He declares, "People and animals aren't the same thing." He is in a space with Fabiola perhaps—God didn't make us like that.

Jean-Charles then addresses his response to Manuelle and Manuelle's initial question:

Manuelle, skin changes.
it's like, the larva, when it was inside the egg,
you, like when you were inside your mother's stomach.
It's like, when you were a little baby. when you were born,
when you were a little baby, you had hardly any hair
didn't that change? don't you have hair?

At this point, the kids explode. Manuelle says that not all babies are born without hair. Marianne wants to distinguish growth from change: "You grow, you don't change," she tells Jean-Charles. Jean-Charles responds to Marianne on the question of change versus growth, saying, "When you were a baby, your eyes were closed." His implication is that clearly they aren't closed anymore; thus she *has* changed. Joanne appeals to the teacher as she points out that Manuelle now and Manuelle as a baby do not look the same—Manuelle has changed. Manuelle then stands up to exclaim, "Do I change my skin like this, vloop, vloop," and she pretends to unzipper her skin and climb out of it.

MAKING CONNECTIONS

Manuelle places on the table the connection between people and insects ("Why, if people eat and eat they don't change their skin, they don't transform, the way insects do?"). Her question is both about changing skin and about the change in form that constitutes metamorphosis. When the other children at first focused on changing skin, Manuelle reminds them that she is thinking also of change of form ("but we don't transform"). In the end, with her "vloop vloop" ("do I change my skin like this, vloop, vloop"), one doesn't know if she is referring only to the movement of a larva emerging out of a whole skin, or if she is also thinking of the transformation from pupa to beetle in this idea of "vloop vloop." In any case, she has introduced the connection to people and she is on the side that there are differences between what these insects do and what humans do—she doesn't think it's the same.

The skin-change question led some children, although not all, to claim the opposite. They remind each other that humans do slough off their skin, playing basketball, as Rudolphe suggested, or inside their clothes, or from sunburn, as another child mentions; and so, having explored a range of examples, they argue that in this case human processes and insect processes are the same—humans change skin, insects do, we all do this.

Jean-Charles represents the broadest usage of *change*. He said, "Manuelle, skin changes," as his opening claim. He then went on to give an example that was not of skin change, but of change of form: The larva is like the embryo. He then added "growing hair," another sign of change that, he seemed to be claiming, was comparable in some way to the changes of metamorphosis. He pointed out to Joanne, when she challenged him by saying, we grow, we don't change, that her eyes were open, and they probably weren't at birth. Jean-Charles seemed to want to use *change* to refer to any number of differences and developments, such as height, more hair, and open eyes, as well as the development from larva to pupa, from embryo to newborn. According to Jean-Charles, all animals, including insects and humans, change over time. He is developing a wealth of feeling for change, but he is seeing all these kinds of change as substantially the same.

CRITIQUE AND REFINEMENT

There are a number of critiques of this broad usage. First, there's Stefan and Fabiola, who simply state that they don't think that people and animals should be compared; they don't think this is a fruitful connection to make. In some sense the whole discussion was a response to this point of view; it was a discussion on the biological plane that asked, In what ways can they be compared?

Both Manuelle and Marianne first pointed out that the examples that Jean-Charles and some of the others were giving were not true without exception; not all people play basketball, not all babies are born without hair, the way—and this part is implicit, unarticulated by the girls—all mealworms move through skin change and metamorphosis. The students' work with mealworms has focused on finding a pattern in the worms' skin changes. The two girls evidently have gained a sense that the word *change* as they want to use it in relation to mealworm growth refers to a sequence that is inviolable, a pattern that is secure and doesn't vary with individuals.

Manuelle critiqued the broad usage of *change* on another front, however, when she argued that changing skin is "vloop vloop," the way a larva gets out of an old skin, not the way old skin gradually is replaced among human beings. As she demonstrated when she pretended to unzip her skin, larva skin is replaced all of a piece.

These students are asking, Is there one kind or more than one kind of change? and, Will one word do or do we need more than one, and what distinctions should they make if we do? They are negotiating what distinctions matter in this context. Certainly Jean-Charles is right: We all change—in some contexts it might even be appropriate to talk about the metamorphosis of a young child into an adult. But what are the crucial features of change in this conversation, with these intentions? The crucial features vary depending on what you want to figure out. In their attempt to understand their mealworms' life cycle, and to understand it in some relation to their own, the children have created a need to sort out a particular version of what *change* might mean.

Although not all the students agree on how the terms should be used at this point, I realize now that they are getting at the basis for the use of the terms *grow* and *develop* in biology. Metamorphic change is a series of distinct stages; it is not a kind of change that is noticeably gradual and continual, like growing over periods of time, as Marianne mentions. Rather, it crucially contains discontinuous stages—"vloop, vloop" and it's over and done. And it follows a reliable pattern—it does not differ from individual to individual like hair growth or the ability or desire to play basketball might.

These students have enjoyed a good first discussion, but how far will their jokes and their wild connections lead them toward truly precise language and clear understanding of the concepts of growth, development, and metamorphosis? Can they learn to use these ideas in scientific thinking? To consider this question, I will explore the following interview with Jean-Charles that took place about a month after the initial conversation.

INTERVIEW WITH JEAN-CHARLES

Jean-Charles, as you remember, was proposing in the discussion a very broad use of the term *change*, which covered everything from the stages of development to the growth of hair and the opening of eyes. He seemed to be making no distinctions, although many of the other children were.

In the interview he was describing a beetle. I will include the Creole because I want to make a point about how he used the grammar of his first language to help himself distinguish the kinds of change in the phenomena in front of him.

> *Li gen yon pakèt de chanjman. Premye chanjman an se lè l te ti bebe li vin gran epi, dezyèm chanjman an li vin toumen yon pupa. Twazyèm chanjman an epi li vin tounen yon beetles.*

> It has a whole bunch of changes. The first change is when it was a baby it got bigger, then, the second change it turned into a pupa. The third change then it turned into a beetle.

Jean-Charles was saying that the beetle goes through a lot of changes. The larva grows, then it gets bigger. And then after a certain period, it turns into first a pupa and then a beetle. He called all these phenomena *chanjman/* changes, reminiscent of his use in the conversation of a broad definition of *change* that included everything from metamorphosis to growing hair. But here he seemed to be making a distinction he didn't make before. I am particularly impressed by the words he chose to make this distinction, which may be a newly acquired or newly relevant distinction for him in this context.

> *vin(i) gran* means "become big" and he uses this for growth.
> *Vin(i) tounen* includes the idea of "becoming" (*vini*) and "of turning into" or "transforming" (*tounen*), and this he uses for *change to another form*.

Jean-Charles used *vini* as a part of both meanings and changes the second term to distinguish the kinds of becoming. There are other Creole words he could have used: He could have used *grandi*/grow for what the larva does, *transfòme*/transform for "turn into"—*transfòme* is what Manuelle used to begin the conversation we explored earlier and *grandi* was used by Joanne, among others, in that conversation. But by including *vini* in both phrases Jean-Charles preserved a sense that, while both "become," one becomes *big* and the other becomes *something else*. The sense of contrast as well as of similarity is represented almost physically in the phrases he chose—one word is common to both phrases, one word is not. Having sorted into two terms these different kinds of change that he perhaps once regarded as essentially the same, he chose by the phrases he constructed to mark also the sense that they are both aspects of the same thing.

Haitian Creole (HC) happens to have in its syntax the capacity to place many verbs next to each other in what are known as serial verb constructions; thus Jean-Charles can say *vini tounen*, literally "become turn into," which sounds quite odd in English. I am suggesting that Jean-Charles makes use of this capacity of HC syntax to explore his developing sense of aspects of change.

Later in the same interview Jean-Charles, of his own volition, switches to English and, in speaking about ants, uses the English terms *grow* and *develop* to work further with these same two aspects of change.

the eggs develop, um, they, the eggs become, um grow,
the eggs growing bigger bigger bigger bigger til it's um develop
and when it's finished it could be a queen or a worker

Here I think Jean-Charles again is constructing his terms, this time in English, to distinguish the types of change he saw within the processes of one organism. He started by saying that the eggs develop, then backtracks to say they grow, which they don't, although the larvae inside, which can be seen, do. The eggs (or actually larvae) grow "bigger, bigger, bigger." This they do "till it's um develop and when it's finished it could be a queen or a worker." When he used "develop" here he was talking about radical changes of form—the change from larva to ant. He used what must for him be a past participle, "develop[ed]," focusing on the over-and-doneness of the change, and he marked this again in the next phrase, "when it's finished." So he doubly marked the sense that the focus in what we call *development* is on the end point. This latter was Manuelle's "vloop vloop" point—some growth is continuous, other is over and done with, vloop vloop. In contrast, when Jean-Charles was referring to continuous growing he used a present participle, "growing," with a comparative, "bigger," and he repeated the comparative three times, "growing bigger bigger bigger." Here I think he was trying to convey his sense of the continuousness of growing, in which the end point is not so much the crucial feature. One can almost get the feeling of the ongoing, time-consuming process as he repeats, "bigger, bigger, bigger." Again I have the strong sense from the way he put these terms together that, in English, as in Creole, Jean-Charles was particularly interested in the way they contrast with each other, the distinctions that they make as a pair. He began, during the whole-class discussion, articulating a rather undifferentiated view of growth; now he has these two aspects of growth, central ones for biology, existing in some sort of defining contrast.

SCIENTIFIC LANGUAGE

Jean-Charles seems to have gained a clearer sense of the difference between what scientists could call "growth" and what they would call "development." Is this a big accomplishment? During the time I spent in Pat and Sylvio's classroom, and the time I spent later on thinking about how to understand what the children were learning, I read a book called *Writing*

Science: Literacy and Discursive Power, by M. A. K. Halliday and James Martin. In this book there is a great deal of discussion about the ways of using language that are characteristic of science. One point made there that seems particularly relevant was the idea that in science, words, and concepts usually exist in relation to each other; that is, scientific terms are seen as parts of frameworks of explanation, which contribute to the definition. For example, you can't understand tension without understanding compression and a theory of forces is implicit in fully understanding them both. The full significance of the terms *invertebrate* and *vertebrate* may require a sense of that separation within evolutionary history; there is often no point in saying that something does not have a backbone unless you understand that some creatures do have a backbone and what follows from this fact. I think Jean-Charles was using, first of all, the language he knows best, HC, and then English, as a tool to map out the territory of growth and development in a similarly broad and conceptual landscape. He has, I think, some distance from these terms—he is aware of them as terms that have their meaning in relation to each other. He has moved from an unexamined everyday usage to a view that suggests an awareness of language itself. He is labeled a special education student, a bilingual student, with particular difficulties with language, and yet he is demonstrating a creative and subtle way of working with words and thought in two languages.

In addition, it is striking that he has found in HC a resource for his developing thought. While it is true that, as a result of its historical usage, HC does not contain a great deal of technical terminology in biology, it still, like any language, is an enormously flexible tool and the potential for clarity is there. There seem to be few limits to the ways in which someone like Jean-Charles who is thinking hard can find to make language work.

Jean-Charles and his fellow students have opened up, for me and for themselves, a concept and explored the requirements for its use in a particular area of science. Although I have shared final data on only one student, I believe that many of these students have developed a view of growth and development, and a way of expressing it, that we would regard as an important part of scientific thinking and scientific language.

IDEAS FOR OTHER CHILDREN

The discussion we just explored was in many ways a rollicking talk. All the thinking and the value that appears when you do an analysis afterward was not obvious at the moment. At the moment, it seemed mainly full of jokes and challenges. That it was allowed to go on was based on trust, the teacher's trust that the students were making sense and making progress. Sylvio, the teacher, trusted that this everyday language, this rollicking talk, and their first language, HC, were adequate, more than adequate, to the task of exploring metamorphosis; he trusted that jokes are part of thinking, that familiar talk in a nonacademic-sounding manner has the capacity for subtlety, that his students were intelligent, had questions and serious intentions, and that they wanted to know. Pat, who had only come to recognize herself as a scientific thinker in her adulthood, waited for the children to make themselves clear. She ignored no idea. She recognized that there was more than one way of constructing the topic.

But Pat and Sylvio also trusted these discussions because they knew I was there making a record of the talk that we could return to. And they trusted these discussions because we had colleagues who would meet together and help to uncover the children's ideas and to consider the next moves.

CHAPTER 8

Keeping It Real

In the movie "ET The Extraterrestrial," there is a scene near the end of the film where the boys and ET are fleeing from the adults who are trying to capture ET. Suddenly they arrive at a clearing and see ET's spaceship hovering overhead. After their initial relief, one of the boys asks, "How's he gonna get up there?" Another answers, "Can't he just beam up?" An older boy gives him a condescending look and replies, "This is the real world."
—Joseph McDonald, *Qualitative Research Design*

The research we do as teachers in our classrooms also matters in the real world. I believe it helps our students. And yet it is unfortunately true that teacher researchers as a community have not had many serious discussions of our methods and their strengths or weaknesses.

How do we know that through our research we are seeing the genuine capacities of our students? How do we know that what we see in our students and what we claim from our work is trustworthy? These are crucial, real-world questions. In this chapter I discuss aspects of teacher research methodology that address these concerns.

EXPLORING CHILDREN'S TALK

The narrative chapters in this book contain many examples of the use of the central methodological practices of teacher research:

1. Stopping time
2. Attending to puzzling moments
3. Expanding the talk

I will not discuss these again here, only ask the reader to recall that these practices are intended to allow us a better understanding of our students' true capacities, especially those of our puzzling students, by helping to provide a more complete view of them and to establish distance from our automatic responses and assumptions. In this chapter I will discuss two parts of a teacher-research project that have a powerful effect on our findings and their value, on the students and for us:

1. Finding a research question
2. Choosing the context in which to collect our data

FINDING A GOOD RESEARCH QUESTION

I am not aware of having a research question as I teach, although I think I used to have them. What I am aware of now is that I collect anything that might be considered thinking or anything that will help me to understand what the children's ideas are and where to go next with them. I write down, whenever I can, all instances of engaged talk, questions I am asked, stories I am told, comments about home, anything that strikes me as odd and serious. It may be that behind this collecting there are many questions that are always there for me, that have become part of the way I listen while teaching. To me it seems, however, that I am just in search of thinking wherever I see it as I am teaching. I am interested in what prompts thinking and curiosity and what I can do to support it. It can be about anything, from apostrophes to gravity.

I do know that, for many of us, particularly as we start out, good questions can focus our attention and in this way they are valuable.

There are many kinds of focusing questions that teacher researchers ask:

How can I get my student writers to revise?
What are the best ways to teach spelling?
Should I allow gunplay in any circumstance?
Why won't my students believe what is said in science books?
How does storytelling help in developing early literacy among bilingual kindergarteners?
Do the girls talk as much as the boys in my discussions?

These are all legitimate and important things to study. However, most questions as first formulated are too narrow, too constraining to our thinking, and too embedded in our own assumptions. What you will think to collect will be too narrow, too thin. You may answer such questions more or less, but without seeing anything really new, without developing a deeper vision, one that challenges you to stay open and learning.

To work with such questions, it is my belief that we have to watch more first, get the feeling of the broader field in which the question operates, for the students and for us; we have to use more of what we know. Let me explain what I mean through an example. This concerns writing and revising.

REVISION AND A FEELING FOR LITERATURE

My friend and colleague Jim Swaim has taught the writing process for years to his third and fourth graders. This account is the result of what he has told me in meetings of the BTRS and what he has written (Swaim, in BTRS, 2004). Jim's students write great fiction, share it and occasionally revise it, learn spelling, punctuation, and a great deal about story structure from what he and they do together. He was nevertheless frustrated that his students didn't seem to see the value in revision and rarely did it unless he explicitly suggested it. He decided to put a tape recorder in the peer conferences he had his students doing, to see what was going on as they tried to revise. What he found distressed him greatly. At one point on the tape he heard two girls conferencing.

> LEE: I don't know. I just have this feeling that I did not put enough detail into it. Do you think I put enough detail or maybe too much?
>
> SUSAN: I think it was pretty good. I mean if you want to change it you can.
>
> LEE: Yeah, I did work really hard but I have a feeling I either put too little or too much detail.
>
> SUSAN: Well, I think in some parts there was too much detail and in some parts there was too little like when you said about the checker and how did they get the checkers?
>
> LEE: I think I'm going to add and put in a page there and stuff. Do you think I should tape all my pages together so that it won't be hard?

SUSAN: No.
LEE: Do you like my story?
SUSAN: Yeah.

His students were successfully using his words about writing and editing. They were using the questions he had taught them to use. But, he felt, they were not applying his principles with any feeling for the story. Their view of literature seemed rote and out of touch with the pleasure of reading and writing.

At the same time Jim was noticing a critical spirit in the writing shares that students did when they wanted to share their work with the larger group. He was disturbed in particular by one experience in which the students were unable to appreciate the playfulness in a story that also contained science misinformation; they focused entirely on the false information.

Jim changed his question as he realized this, from, How can I teach them to revise or what happens when they revise? to:

Where do I see an honest response to literature among my students?

This second question was a different sort of question. It was much broader and at the same time more fundamental. What was an honest response and when did it occur? He didn't assume he knew exactly what such a response would look like. This question made him explore his own feeling for literature—what did he respond to and how, why did he read and write? At the same time this question led him to collect and document, in tape recordings and field notes, the range of responses he heard from his students about their reading and writing. This was a search in which Jim was partly wondering what he was looking for. He became more of a watcher, observing his students as they read and wrote. This is the sort of question that, I believe, has more potential to teach us about our students and their possibilities for genuine involvement with the curriculum. It includes us as people and as participants.

In fact, as Jim watched, he did learn a great deal. A new story genre developed in Jim's writer's workshop. The students began to participate in one another's stories, by suggestions to the author and then, in some cases, as actual actors in dramatizations. Collaboration with others became part of writing workshop in a new way.

Hannah developed stories in which everyone was welcome to offer suggestions. Revision happened as kids entered her stories with their ideas, and in fact she ended up writing her classmates into her stories as characters. Sometimes they would act out the stories. This style led to a great deal of diversion from the main story line and occasional confusion, but also to clever and enjoyable stories.

One of Hannah's stories developed into a group project, written and then acted out and including the family dog and every single one of the 12 girls in that third-grade class. It was an uninhibited, raucous, loud, clever performance that literally had the boys rolling on the floor when it was viewed by the class.

However, this new style did not work for everyone. Jim also had a student named Jonathan who wrote very well technically, and loved to write and to share his writing, but nobody wanted to collaborate with Jonathan. Jonathan did not appreciate getting suggestions. His stories were always about the successful exploits of a superhero. However, there was little if any obstacle for the superhero to overcome.

> He turned around to see the Karate King Army attacking a boy. Combat Man started fighting. In a minute most of the army was dead. The rest retreated to their hideout.

Jim asked himself, what does Jonathan get from this new type of collaborative writing in his classroom? His fellow students told him that his were not really stories, that heroes need obstacles to overcome. He would agree, but he never seemed to change his stories. They pointed out to him that he never took their suggestions. His literary style mirrored his social situation. He was an isolated child and was so inflexible that changes in schedule could lead to screaming fits.

Jim worried about Jonathan and occasionally had to protect him from his classmates' criticism. He also took notes about the role of writing in the social life of his classroom, and he found and explored ways to support it. Later in the year Jim notes a story that Jonathan shared in which the main character, a 10-year-old named Jon, suffers a wide range of indignities, all amazingly relevant to Jonathan's own life experience. In the sharing sessions that ensued, the audience almost gleefully offered Jonathan suggestions aimed at making the main character's life even more pathetic and tragic, all of which, for a change, Jonathan appeared to enjoy. After Hannah had made one such suggestion, Jonathan commented:

My compliments to Hannah. One thing I can say about you is that
you are always weird and I like that in you. I wish we all could be
that way.

This is a moving moment in Jonathan's life in this classroom. He seems
to have learned something important. But I didn't mean to tell this story to
show that Jim did the right thing as a teacher. It's rather about how Jim's
question changed and what Jim was able to see as a result. Jim's question
started with irritation and concern about the technique of revision within
writing process pedagogy and how his students were taking it up. Many
productive questions start from irritation, in my experience. As it broadened, it led him to create some distance from his teaching and the ideas
about and techniques for revision that he had grown used to. As he said, it
was no longer obvious to him what he should be doing. The familiar pattern of writers' workshop was disrupted and opened to question. He began
to watch the children and also to observe himself in order to reconnect with
his own knowledge and experience of literature. He noticed who writers'
workshop was working for, and also he also learned from children, such
as Jonathan, who did not embrace it so easily. His question grew from these
experiences.

Has Jim ever really answered his question? Does Jim now know how
to teach revision? Yes and no. He has learned many things, but it turns out
that this question is not really a question that you answer. It's developed
into a very big question, a question that you teach with, that keeps you
observing all sorts of children, considering and reconsidering your experience of literature and its place in your life and theirs. It's a question that
keeps teaching connected to the real world.

THE POWER OF CONTEXT

When you have chosen a focusing question, you may begin to collect data
on this question. Where you collect that data will determine how your
question changes and develops. I think it is very important that we take
data from multiple contexts. We should not just stick to the obvious place
where what we are interested in is supposed to happen. If you are interested in cooperative learning, you must look for instances of cooperation
elsewhere than in the activities that we provide. That way you will come
to understand more of what cooperation might mean and develop a broader

sense of what situations support it. If you are interested in fantasy play, observe it in every place you can. You will come to understand much more about the functions and pleasures it contains. Many engaged in research, academic research and teacher research as well, make the mistake of defining what they are looking for before they have carefully observed. The research is then focused on a narrow view of the activity or skill.

If we are interested in whether children can use evidence when they argue in science, for example, we must watch them argue on the playground or other places where they care about the result. Concluding that students of a certain background or below a certain age or intelligence cannot, for example, argue from evidence is a mistake that some academic research has made because it looked in only one context. The validity that we care about, conclusions based on the true abilities of our students, requires that we not make the same mistake. Looking in multiple contexts is crucial because it gives us a more complex and truer sense of our students' abilities.

As you choose different contexts, a variable of great importance that you will want to attend to is the amount of control your students have in one context compared with another. It became a maxim in the BTRS that if you want to understand children's ideas and motivations, if you truly want to see them thinking, you must watch the situations in which they have more control. The children in Jim Swaim's writing group were able to show him different motives for revision and different ways to do it because they were given more control than usual. In the following example, data collection extends to out-of-school time.

Cindy Beseler was a special education teacher with students who were considered developmentally delayed; these were 16- and 17-year-olds who were outside the regular high school program, learning instead a primary grade curriculum. Part of what they did was job training. Cindy took them to work at a local hospital where they were paid for stuffing envelopes. One aspect of her responsibility in this area was to help them understand what to say in public: Whom to talk to on the subway, for example. What was appropriate to say and what was not to coworkers, to the supervisor. They sometimes revealed family secrets to total strangers or failed to respond to a simple "How are you?" She was trying to teach them what to say where.

Cindy and the students arrived at the hospital every Friday after a ride on public transportation. Once there, Cindy would let down her guard. The students at this point would start to talk differently. They would make noises, say childish things, act silly. Cindy wasn't totally comfortable, but she could sense that they were and she kind of enjoyed it. She felt bad telling them to stop, so rather than continue to teach appropriate behavior, she taped their talk. Looking over the tape at leisure she learned that her students had language skills she had not before recognized. Here, for example, is part of a conversation on drinks for the prom they were planning:

1. Bill: Scotch on the rocks, if you need ice.
2. Rebecca: You're supposed to say Pepsi on the rocks.
3. Douglas: How about Roxanne Pepsi on the rocks?
4. Bill: How about Diet Pepsi on the rocks?
5. Rebecca: How about Cindy on the rocks? How about Cindy on the rocks?
6. Douglas: Diet Cindy Pepsi on the rocks?
7. Rebecca: Ah yes, that's even better.
8. Douglas: Diet Kosher Pepsi Cindy on the rocks.

Rebecca knows there's no alcohol at the prom. Roxanne is another teacher and Douglas makes a play on "the rocks" and "Roxanne." Then they add "Cindy," since she also is a teacher. Next they turn it into Diet Pepsi, since one of their number has diabetes. "Kosher" is added for a student who keeps kosher. This play with language is both clever and inclusive, socially sensitive.

From the subway and the classroom, she had seen what they could *not* do. Obviously this was important information, but in this context, where they were in control, she was able to explore their intentions with language, the skills and purposes they were interested in developing. At the end of one of these playful talks in which they were remembering their elementary school, Cindy heard one boy say to another,

ARNOLD: You know then you have a learning disability?
BILL: No.
ARNOLD: Me neither . . . I know now!
BILL: Yeah!
ARNOLD: Now I know I special needs.

These students first demonstrate the pleasure they take in language. Next they use their language to share grief, certainly a central part of mature language abilities. My point is that these situations in which the students have more control than in many instructional contexts are often a crucial corrective to assumptions we make about what students know or can do. The situations in which their intentions are paramount—and these situations can be in the playground but they can also be in a class discussion in which the teacher follows their lead, they can be private conversations, small-group discussions, even chance conversations with students walking down the hall—often allow us to see the students' abilities differently. These experiences are especially important in regard to language—many students who are considered to have language deficits have strengths that we are blind to in many classroom contexts. In addition, looking at various contexts deepens our own understanding of what language is and what it is for. Without this perspective, would we have looked at how the students used language to discuss their own disabilities? Were we aware of the place of grief in the functions of language?

These experiences have led Cindy Beseler to teach and research now always with the questions, What do my students know how to do already? What is important to them? What can I do to provide a context that will support these abilities and interests? What is the relationship between what feels right and natural and important to my students and what I can learn from that, and what I have to tell them to do? She teaches with this inquiry in mind. For our research to help us to see into the true abilities of our students, it is essential to look in more than just the obvious place.

CONCLUSION

As ET's human friend says, this is the real world. Our studies should connect us, and allow us to connect our students, to the largest world of thought that we can manage. We must challenge ourselves to see beyond what we assume, beyond what we see at first. Our questions are not classroom questions. They are not simple questions. They are human questions and involve us, the wider world, and all that our students can bring to the pleasure of learning.

CHAPTER 9

Djeissen's Question

Written with *Djeissen da Pina, Paula da Silva, Angelica Mourato, Fabio da Freitas, Anderson Lima, Elisa Mirando, Rodolfo Bonates, David Dutra, and Marc daCosta*

> Understanding starts with a question, not any question but a real question. A question that, because it is real, does not remain detached from us . . . a real question expresses a desire to know.
> —Bettencourt, A., *On Understanding Science*
> [quoted by Van Tassel in Well, 2001]

When a young boy from Cape Verde in my seventh-grade science class asked one day, "Why do the roads in Cape Verde fall in and become ruined?" I didn't have any idea what we would do with such a question. But I did know we would do something with it. Paula, another Cape Verdean, had reiterated Djeissen's question. Fabio and Rodolfo, two Brazilian classmates of his, had joined enthusiastically in the short discussion we had that day about it, miming and laughing about the bumpiness of the ride along some of the roads they knew in Brazil. There was some excitement about this topic. But more than that, the cue for me was the boy himself. Djeissen had arrived 3 years earlier from Cape Verde, unable to read and write. He was intelligent, and was now literate, but he was at a serious disadvantage in many academic areas and I was worried that, now, at 13, he was showing signs that his commitment to school was beginning to suffer. I would follow his question for him because he needed me to. But equally important, I knew there would be no loss to others from my following his question. From the research I have done and reported on in this book, I was sure that by following a question like his, a real question placed deep in his life and his concerns, every child in the class, and I as well, would learn with and from him.

THE ACHIEVEMENT GAP

As I began to write the story of Djeissen's question, the results of the state tests came out. Again many schools are in trouble, having failed to score adequately. I hear much discussion of the reasons for and solutions to the poor performance of particular groups of students—African American children, poor children, immigrant children. I know that there are many causes of the achievement gap, some having to do with the tests themselves (Hudicourt-Barnes, Noble, O'Connor, Rosebery, Suarez, Warren, & Wright, 2008). But in addition to critiquing the test, and even the idea of such tests, I also hear us talking at times like these about the learning difficulties that children have whose families don't or can't help them and of the problems that poverty and stress create in children's ability to learn. Again I know there is truth to this. These are problems we must address as a society. But, as I have tried to show in this book, it has been my experience that many of the children we are talking about in this way have important and even sophisticated ideas as well as normal or above-normal capacity to think about them. They have been thinking hard about many things. They are not behind in all the ways we sometimes think they are. I wrote this book because I believe the practices of teacher-research contain methods to help us recognize the intellectual lives and intellectual liveliness of students whose ideas and experiences may not be familiar to us. This chapter gives further proof of this belief.

In this chapter I take a longer look at a particular case of teaching and learning than I did in the other chapters; I describe here a good deal of what the children did, said, and wrote as they worked on Djeissen's question, and some of what they learned and learned how to do over the course of several months. I do not present this story as an exemplary piece of curriculum. Curriculum is always a work in progress, shaped by interaction with particular students, by other events, and by one's own always changing understanding. As I explain below, there are many things I would do differently next time, and probably other things that would go differently. Rather, I include this final chapter because, with its more detailed descriptions of events that took place over time, I hope it offers a fuller demonstration of how a teacher research approach to the children's ideas gives the children—all the children—a chance to experience themselves as thinkers, both privately and on a public stage and gives the teacher the opportunity to use their ideas as resources. The children's ideas are front and center, and for good reason—they are serious ideas. In conjunction with my goals and my knowledge, their ideas will determine what the class learns and does next. Their backgrounds and experiences are not lacking, are not deficient; rather they contain resources that support them in effective thinking and learning and support me in teaching them.

I ask the reader to notice the children's ability to observe and to ask difficult questions based on their observations. I ask the reader to observe the children's ability to challenge generalizations and refine models to suit specific situations. I ask the reader to notice the broad connections they make, sometimes extremely broad, and the way these connections push our thinking. I ask the reader to notice the initiative they take, the life of the mind they reveal.

INTRODUCING THE CHILDREN

This story took place while I was teaching science in a two-way Portuguese bilingual program; in this program the children were taught some subjects in Portuguese and others in English. I taught science in English. The students I will speak about here were in the seventh grade. Some came from Brazil and some from Cape Verde and some were born in the United States, but their families were from the Azores or Angola or other Portuguese-speaking countries. There were native Portuguese speakers among them and others for whom English was their first language, but Portuguese was the language of their heritage. The Cape Verdean children sometimes spoke only Cape Verdean Creole when they arrived, a language similar to but also significantly different from Portuguese. The children varied widely in the amount of education their parents had received; some parents had received hardly any, while some were highly educated in either Portuguese or English. Some children, like Djeissen, were here with uncles or grandparents, receiving an education and a different kind of chance, while their parents remained in their country of origin. They helped me to reconstruct and to understand what we had done together, and for this reason, they are included as coauthors for this chapter.

QUESTIONS

I had a wall in the classroom where I wrote down the questions my students asked that we couldn't easily answer. We began the year studying the trees in our courtyard garden. We drew the leaves, categorized the different leaf shapes, and matched each tree to descriptions in a field guide. We noticed that we had both evergreens and deciduous trees. Marc asked if the evergreens' needles had veins like the veins they had observed in the leaves. We dissected some needles, with the help of a botanist friend of mine, and observed through the microscope that they did indeed have veins. Gilberto wondered why the needles didn't fall off in the winter. He was able to find a passage in an encyclopedia that gave some reasons for this. As we went on to chemistry, children asked questions about whether carbon ever disappeared, and why oxygen combined with so many other elements and about what fire did. Questions like Djeissen's, however, were not specifically related to what we were doing in science on a daily basis and these we had to save for later study. We wrote it on the wall and left it there. The children reminded me a number of times about it—they too seemed to see it as significant, not to be forgotten—until, during the winter, when we had completed our required study of chemistry, we decided to start.

What you will read below does not include everything we did, but it does present some activities and conversations in some detail. While I hope this level of detail is not confusing or tedious, I chose it because I think it demonstrates more clearly how and what the students were thinking. I also occasionally use hindsight to add my reflections on things I notice now that I did not notice then, on what seemed to work and what seemed not to, and what I would do differently next time. These reflections are in italics.

WHY DO THE ROADS IN CAPE VERDE COLLAPSE?

I figured this was a study of erosion. What I love about all levels of earth science is the feeling of seeing through time. If you know what you are looking at, or if you are with someone who does, you can see evidence of erosion or glaciers, or of volcanoes, of dried-up rivers or even oceans, all kinds of long-ago events. I hoped that my students would begin to feel the thrill of this kind of experience. At the same time I hoped that they would learn some practical ideas that might address the problem of erosion on Cape Verde, or anywhere else. I wanted them to see erosion not as just the way it is, but as something that study and scientific thinking might provide an answer to. In addition I was hoping that they would become familiar with a range of new vocabulary and an experimental approach to such questions and that they would see the value of creating models to explore the way soil and rocks might act in the real world.

Models

I read up on Cape Verde. The encyclopedia and Web resources I was able to find mentioned sandy soil, lack of vegetation, and steep mountains as significant causes for erosion. We began with the issue of sandy soil. Each team of children took two big aluminum foil roasting pans and filled one with sand and one with soil. They put three books under one end of each pan so that the pans rested at an angle. They then made a hole in the lower end. They poured water into cups with holes in them to simulate rain. They made it rain over each pan and then collected the soil and sand and water that were swept through the hole. They filtered out the water and measured the sand using measuring spoons.

The results showed that more sand was carried out of the pans than soil. Sand eroded more easily. However, we had to redo the sand and soil erosion pans when David realized that we might not have poured the same amount of water on each pan. We redid the experiment again, keeping the amount of rain constant. Again we measured the water and the soil that traveled down with the water. And again we found that sand eroded more easily.

In the next round, we varied the steepness of the pans to see how that changed the amount of erosion. Again we measured the water and soil that flowed through the hole at the bottom of the roasting pan. The results showed that the steeper the slope of the pan, the more soil or sand eroded.

Looking for Solutions

I told the students that scientists thought that plants would prevent some erosion, so we decided to add another roasting pan and fill it with soil and plants. I asked them to predict what they thought would happen before we tried the experiment. Paula wrote that she didn't think the plants would help "because when it rains the big rain will take the plants with it." Angelica thought that plants were attached to the dirt and so they would go together. Others thought the plants would stabilize the land. Marc said that the plants would drink the water, which would keep it from carrying off the soil. David and Marc imagined the roots as holding on to the soil or sand as the water goes by and thus preventing some erosion.

Reflections

I was slightly surprised and disappointed by Paula and Angelica's predictions. To me it seemed obvious that the roots would prevent some erosion. Still I was challenged by their various ways of imagining the role of roots. Marc's ideas, that the plants drink water, seemed sort of naive, but later he explained to me that he meant over time the plants would use water and keep it from accumulating. I realized I wasn't entirely sure what the roots really do, only that they help.

We set up the experiment, roasting pans with plants and pans without. After we measured what eroded, we saw that the pans with plants suffered as much erosion as the plants without. We were puzzled. Especially me. Angelica then noticed a problem with experimental design—she pointed out that the soil containing the plants was already wet—we had transplanted well-watered classroom plants into the pan and they came with their own damp soil. We were adding water to soil that was already somewhat saturated. We decided to plant some grass seed in another roasting pan and after it came up, we let the soil dry out somewhat. We then tried the experiment again. This time the results showed that the grass prevented some erosion.

The Ribeiras

Had we found a solution for Cape Verde? Djeissen said no. On this point, he later wrote: "We thought we should put plants and rock on the side of the road. It did work but when we put we forgot that in Cape Verde rains very heavy and that the ribeira get full of water. Ribeiras are like rivers but they start coming from the mountain and until the ocean. The ribeira gets so strong when it rains a lot, that it carries big animals sometimes. It can break bridges. You can imagine how much dirt it can carry."

Here Djeissen explained that the vegetation on Cape Verde was not strong enough to withstand the kinds of rains they have there. Paula's earlier comment that big rains can carry plants away now made sense to me. Her prediction was based on what she had seen. Our experiment had shown one thing, but the actual situation was more complicated.

A Note on Ribeira

The Cape Verdean children were determined to retain the word in Portuguese. At first I was puzzled by their usage. I got a Portuguese-English dictionary and told them that the word meant "river" in English. Later I realized that they did not feel they could use the English word "river" to convey what they meant. To them the word ribeira *signified a river that can change hugely during the rainy season. They explained to me that many ribeiras begin as ditches up in the mountains near the top of the volcano on Fogo, the island they are from. Then, when the rains come, they fill and eventually overflow. The river near our school is the same all the time, with only minor variation, and it is rarely violent in any way.*

Different Kinds of Rain

From what the children were telling me about the ribeiras, I realized I knew very little about what the rain was like in Cape Verde. We looked up a rain table and compared it with a rain table for Boston. This one (see Figure 9.1) includes Paula's notes.

From this we realized that in Cape Verde all the year's rain takes place in a very few weeks. Comparing this chart to one for Boston, we could see what a different pattern this was. We tried to model the two different kinds of rain. Now we used a spray bottle for light rain and a cup with big holes to simulate the heavy rain in Cape Verde. Using our pans again, we found that heavy rain carries a great deal more sand and soil than does light rain. Anderson and Marc wrote:

The light rain didn't do much but make holes, 1 T of sand [that eroded]. Heavy rain was a big difference. There was 20 T of sand [that eroded]. There were more holes and made rivers.

Reflections

I was expecting only measurements of how much sand was carried off. That is what we had done with our roasting pan experiments before. The difference Anderson and Marc noted in what the rain did to the soil or to the sand really added to the story. These two children noticed, and I

Figure 9.1. Yearly Rainfall in Cape Verde (in millimeters)

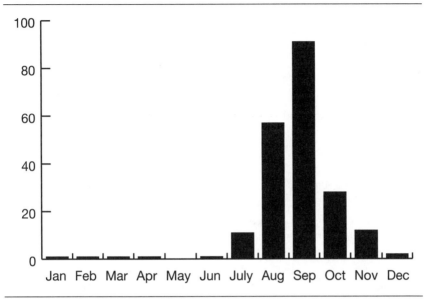

Jan Feb Mar Apr May Jun July Aug Sep Oct Nov Dec

Paula's notes: All the rain is in August and September. It does rain more in the U.S. but it doesn't seem like it because in the U.S. it is all spread out over the year. And some is snow in Boston. Percipitation means rain and snow.

Source: CapeVerdeinfo.org.uk

didn't, that ribeira were created in the pans with heavy rain and that this didn't happen with the light rain.

Getting down Among the Grains of Sand

Why should the sand erode more easily than the dirt? We didn't know. So next I provided sand and soil. Each team of students had a jar with each. We watched and drew what happened when we poured water into them. Then we put the sand and the soil together into a jar of water. Later we looked at both sand and soil under the microscope. We were trying to see for ourselves what is different about sand and soil and what water does when it comes into contact with them. Paula observed that when the water hit the sand, it made a "hole of erosion." David and Djeissen were handling the soil and commented that there was something sticky about it that was different from sand. They said that the soil seemed to hold on to other soil, but the sand did not—Rodolfo added that this was especially true when water was added. Fabio then wanted to know how sand could hold on to sand, or how soil held on to soil. Laughing, he pointed out, "They don't have hands." Rodolfo noticed that there was more space between the pieces of sand than between the pieces of soil. David thought that the sand was harder. When you look at sand under the microscope, you see small rocks, he said. David thought that the sand was made of hard minerals and the soil was not and that this made a difference in stickiness.

Reflections

I love when someone makes a remark like Fabio's, "They don't have hands." He wasn't confused—he was asking a genuine question: How does soil stick together? I think the metaphors we often have to use to talk about natural phenomenon are one area that fascinates children. Fabio was keeping his engagement playful in noting that the soil does not have hands, but at the same time he was refusing to accept a statement—they hold on to each other—because he could not really understand it.

David and Djeissen's idea of the soil's "stickiness" is something I would like to follow up on. What allows damp dirt to stick together so differently from sand? I had never wondered before. A botanist friend I shared this with told me that this was an important idea—but it was not one I could get up to speed on very quickly. Maybe next time.

We also observed that when you put sand and soil together in a jar of water the soil stays up in the water for a long time, while the sand sinks immediately. Rodolfo noticed that the soil even feels dry while it is on top of the water. The children had worked on the idea of density in physical science; they jumped at the explanation that the soil is less dense and the sand goes down more quickly because it is more dense. David, however, pointed out that the soil didn't fall as fast as the sand, but it did fall eventually. After a few minutes it fell, and he wondered why it took so long. Anderson suggested that the dirt might have sucked in some water and that way gotten denser over time. We continued to wonder why sand eroded more in our experiments than soil did—if sand is more dense, then it should be harder for the water to carry it, not easier. Then Paula told me a story: "There is a weak tree. It bends with the wind. It stays rooted during a big storm. In the same place there is also a stronger tree there too. It won't bend with the wind. The big storm uproots it entirely." The sand is like that, she thought.

Reflections

I try not to feel that I have to understand every question or every idea; but I do keep track of them. I don't know why the soil can float, and then eventually sink. Anderson, thinking that the soil could suck in water and thus become more dense, was on an interesting track, but I didn't understand very clearly what he meant. During our study of density, we had discussed less dense things as having "less stuff" on the inside—maybe that was on his mind.

I was intrigued by Paula's story. She was seeing some relationship. I should have made it the focus of a group discussion in order to understand better what the relationship she saw was.

Different Sand and Close Observation

Djeissen next objected that the sand in Cape Verde was different. As he worked with the sand I had provided he told us that the sand in Cape Verde was not so rough and rocky as the sand we were using, which came from a rough-water cove in Rockport, Massachusetts. In order to model Cape Verde more accurately, I got some sand from a beach in Chatham, Massachusetts. The children wanted terms to distinguish the two types of sand and so we chose the word *finer* for the Chatham sand, which had smaller particles and was smoother, and *rougher* for the Rockport sand. *Finer* was a new word for the students and was consequently hard for them to remember until they realized that it had a Portuguese cognate.

David and Djeissen decided to compare the holes that the water made in the two kinds of sand. They noticed that the finer sand seemed to absorb the rain like soil did. They showed other children and the class discussed the differences. They said that the rocky sand didn't look like it was sucking the water in. It looked like the water was just passing through. Paula thought the softer, finer sand and also the soil almost swelled up when the water got into them.

Some kids thought we should try another experiment comparing hard rocky sand with soft sand to see which eroded more easily and how it looked.

Reflections

Their observations here were very helpful in seeing the difference that the size of the particle makes. The finer the sand, the closer it is to being soil, as we learned later.

In their notebooks I see their wish compare the erosion between the two kinds of sand—some of them had written down this idea there and in preparing to write this chapter I found it—but it did not stand out for me at the time. We did not do this experiment. I wish I had noticed their proposal then. Who knows what I was worrying about instead?—perhaps the eighth grade, which was not behaving well for me. Still I am pleased even now to see their growing feeling for the role of experiments.

Now we were interested in the differences between kinds of sand. We took the rough sand from Rockport and separated it into the different kinds of things we found in it. We found bits of shells and what seemed to be teeth, maybe fish teeth, and we found what seemed to be bits of rocks. We also found tiny pieces of plastic, maybe from some toy. Could this all count as sand? Angelica and Elisa started imagining how bigger things might become small enough to become sand. We looked at a piece of sandstone with a hand lens to see the grains of sand that constituted it, and we also scratched some granite with another rock until some tiny grains came loose from it, creating new sand. For homework the students wrote how they imagined a beach might be created.

They wrote about rocks being hit by pebbles and waves and wind, about rivers and ribeiras carrying sand down from the mountains, about shells and skeletons falling to the sand below and eventually breaking up from the action of the waves, about plants growing and dying in the ocean. They included the role of swimmers and beachgoers and fish and boats as well as waves and wind.

Reflection

The homework was handed in by every child. When everyone does their homework, I take it as a sign that the work has made sense to them and that they are enjoying their thinking.

Trees Losing Leaves

Rodolfo and Anderson then suggested that it might be important that more trees lose their leaves here than in Cape Verde. There are deciduous trees there, but there is no season of bare trees as in New England. What do the leaves do for the soil? When we discussed this idea, Paula thought that the fallen leaves "kind of keep the water there so it won't carry a lot of the dirt with it." Angelica watched the water hit the leaves in a pan with soil and dirt. She wrote, "When they are on the ground and it rains the leaves kind of protect the soil."

But Djeissen added that there are many different kinds of leaves and they do different things. We were sure that, because there were fewer deciduous trees in Cape Verde, there were also fewer leaves falling to the ground, but we didn't know much about exactly what kinds of trees grew there. However, we were able to bring in various leaves from our own area to observe in what different ways they would act as barriers to erosion from the rain.

Reflections

> *Angelica's use of the idea of protection helped me to imagine what the leaves do to prevent some erosion. I noticed also that Djeissen often rejects the broad generalization. He is always thinking of exceptions. He seems to feel a sort of ownership over the details of Cape Verde. His comments about different kinds of leaves and different kinds of sand are part of what leads us into the intricacies of the process. What can be different about sand? What do leaves of different shapes and thickness do differently? His concerns have been invaluable.*

EROSION ELSEWHERE: BEYOND THE ROASTING PAN

From what the children were saying in class one day I suddenly realized that they thought of erosion as happening only in Cape Verde. It was Cape Verde's problem. They hadn't considered that it might take place elsewhere, nor had I thought to make that clear. In a class discussion the next day I asked them to consider whether erosion happened everywhere, and they did begin to wonder—but they concluded only that maybe there was erosion some other places, but not everywhere. We had a field trip planned to a glacial kettle pond in our area and when I mentioned this concern to the science coordinator, she arranged to focus some of the trip on the efforts currently being made to prevent erosion of the surrounding land into the pond. When we went there we observed some of their techniques, placing trees perpendicular to the line of erosion, planting vegetation. Most memorable, however, was an unplanned demonstration. During the week of the field trip it had been snowing and during the course of the morning, as we toured the pond, some snow melted. The melted snow flowed down the paths we were walking on, carrying sand and soil to the pond; we could see the rivulets of erosion as it traveled. The paths looked in some places just like our roasting pans after we poured water on them. The dirt and sand from the path was being carried by the snowmelt into the pond. "Now we know there is erosion in the U.S.!" wrote Marc.

Angelica had been seeking an image on the Web of the hot springs in the Azores that she had visited. We had read some material on volcanoes and had discussed the volano on Fogo as a source for the rocks and soil there; Angelica had told us that there were volcanoes in the Azores as well and the spring was right next to an old volcano. She and her family would picnic there, cooking food by putting it in a bag and lowering it into the hot water— the heat, she suggested, must be coming from underneath the earth.

After we saw erosion at the pond, and realized that it took place every-where, it occurred to Angelica that there might be images on the Web of erosion in other countries, too. Angelica printed some images she found and then Fabio and Rodolfo went to work to find pictures of erosion in Brazil.

Fabio found a picture of an enormous canyon. The surrounding land appeared to lack vegetation entirely. He wrote: "This is what erosion in Brazil is like. It look like a canyon but it was made by erosion. In Brazil some places my mother says there not enough plants to hold the soil. And some erosions in Brazil are deep and big, and sometimes is really scary. In my grandmother's house it was raining a lot so the land cracked opened."

Fabio found images on the Web that showed the cracks and canyons he remembered. The images he found from Brazil were from an area of much flatter land than that of Fogo, the volcanic island the Cape Verdean children were from. We weren't sure we completely understood how they were formed, since the land looked so flat. One of our kindergarten teach-ers is from Brazil and, it turned out, she knew a botanist in Brazil. We e-mailed him and he told us that the rain was so hard and the land so free of vegetation in some places that big canyons and gullies did form very quickly. However, with Fabio's memories confirmed, we did not pursue any further what caused these formations. This was a case where I felt that to try to understand fully some of the ideas they were bringing up would have led us too far ahead of what I knew or could quickly learn.

Reflections

At first Fabio realized the power of erosion to make a canyon like the one he saw. He may have had the idea, though, that not all landforms are created. "It look like a canyon but it was made by erosion"—if this were a real canyon, he seemed to be saying, it would not have been "made by erosion." As other children shared their images and their ideas about what had caused them, Fabio began to recognize that every landform has a history, some process that created its particular characteristics.

A month or so later, Elisa and Paula came running in from the playground after a rain saying they had found erosion there. We all went outside and they showed us a sandy spot on the ball field with rivulets and also big wet footprints. Elisa and Paula wrote: "One day we were playing outside and it had just finished raining, so that had made erosion. We went to a baseball field and there we saw erosion on the field. We think that when the rain came so strong, the sand got indented and this caused the erosion. We also think that when the rain fell, it slid down as a river, and it pushed the sand down with it, and that caused the erosion."

Reflections

I was delighted by their connection to the playground. This was a fairly flat and sandy playground. The girls saw that the rain caused an indentation. How did it do this? Perhaps they thought that the rain pushed the sand grains closer together and so they took up less space. And also that the rain carried some sand away with it. I wish I had thought to ask and to explore further.

This is again a moment where I felt they were there, down among the grains of sand, asking questions and noticing things I had never thought of.

From this time on, kids made very wide connections. They wondered about erosion of the blacktop on the playground—could the wind, scuffing shoes, the pebbles blown across it cause this substance to erode? They wondered about what tree roots did under their sidewalks—how did they make the big bumps that they encountered as they walked? They wondered about vibration—in some spots in their neighborhoods you could feel the ground shake when a big truck drove by. What did this do to the soil?

Marc became fascinated with wind and its role in erosion. He found some cement that had eroded near his house—the effect, he thought, of wind and people walking. Anderson found an image on the Web of a beach at the bottom of a cliff and suggested that the process of making this beach involved sand from two sources: Some arrived from the mountains in a river or in runoff from a storm, but also the action of waves might pull soil and sand from the cliffs along the shore. Anderson wanted to try this experimentally; as he wrote, "A project that we hope to do is grabbing a roasting pan, put dirt inside of the pan, put water, and also make waves like in Cape Verde on top to see if there will be erosion."

MAKING SOIL

Thinking about leaves led Rodolfo to wonder about how over time the leaves will turn into soil. Rodolfo had studied decomposition in sixth grade and told me that he had long wanted to know how long it took. We buried some of the leaves we found in our courtyard in small containers of dirt to see how long they would take to decompose. We also put other things in, pieces of paper, bark, and plastic, to see if they would turn into soil as well. There was much speculation on what would help the process. We added water to one container and not to another to see if that made a difference. We added worms in one container and not another. We wondered also what could change. Could plastic someday turn into little pieces of soil? Could paper?

I asked the children to write for homework how they thought soil was made. This was another homework that everyone did.

Djeissen shared his ideas the next morning: "I don't know how you say, when trees undo it . . . when they old, they start undoing. [I offer the word *decompose*] yes, decomposing, when water hit soil, you know how leaves, when rains, they break. And bark too. And rocks, they decompose in a lot of time. . . . There are places where there are leaves, and then after a while it's gone."

Reflections

I like Djeissen's use of "undoing"—it felt to me that he was talking about the cyclic nature of all this. Leaves are made; then their structure is undone and the pieces return to soil. Rocks also can be undone, he says— but in this case we would not call it decomposition, but erosion. He is seeing these processes as analogous, perhaps both covered by the term "undo." I wish I had made the connection between the two processes, and the differences, explicit.

After a discussion that included worms, dead bodies, and garbage and bacteria, Paula asked, "Could diamonds become part of soil?" She thought if there was enough time even diamonds could.

Reflections

This is the sort of extreme case that the children often surprise me with. The children knew that diamonds were tremendously hard. But if everything had been made up of other things, made up of elements, as we had discussed when we were doing chemistry, then can everything "undo"— even something as hard as a diamond?

Paula's question became the homework for the next night. Anderson begins with his ideas the following morning : "Diamonds are so hard you can't cut them. They are special. Rocks will turn into gravel, finer gravel. And finer gravel will turn into finer gravel. But not into soil."

David then suggested that, for some things, the idea was absurd, "if *anything* can become soil, how about a drink? I mean *become* soil, not go into soil. A drink goes into soil. How about paper? I had a piece of paper a few years ago and it is still the same. . . . I have had a rock for five years and it looks like sand but it is still the same as it used to be." When he looked at it recently, it "was covered in something. It looked like sand. It was whitish yellow, on some parts, but not all."

Marc next listed some things that change: Water changes to vapor; fire burns and diamonds too could change, but, he claimed, they would not become soil—they would change to sand. Djeissen said the little pieces of diamond were too hard to become dirt. He agreed it would have to be sand, but that over time it could happen. Next Angelica, like Marc, presented a list of ways things that can change: metal can rust, plastic can fall apart, and cloth can rot. "A lot of things can change," she stated.

Reflection

I was struck by their wish to put the idea that a diamond could change into soil into the context of many other kinds of change. Angelica, Marc, and David all invoke various kind of change. I would never have thought of doing this. It seemed to help them see the possibilities. I will do it in the future.

Angelica then brought up the idea of a diamond scratching a diamond; if this happened, she proposed, then the little piece that was scratched off could become part of the dirt. Rodolfo reiterated this difficult idea: "Only a diamond can scratch a diamond, and that little piece could become dirt." David asked, "So anything can become soil?" Paula said, "Eventually."

But would it become sand or soil? They asked me to find out the answer for sure. I contacted a geologist, who told us that the difference between sand and soil is technically only the size of the grain; if the piece of diamond was small enough it could be considered soil. I am not sure that the children completely accepted this. They had seen sand in the microscopes and it shines like a diamond. They did, however, remember the very fine sand from the beach in Chatham, Massachusetts; this, they had observed in their experiments earlier, acted more like dirt.

CONCLUDING THOUGHTS

As their concluding activity the children made a PowerPoint of erosion in Cape Verde and elsewhere. They searched the Web for images of erosion on beaches and mountains and roads and then wrote their explanations for each of them. Their conversation and their writing about these images served as an assessment for me of the ways they had learned to think about land and the processes that create it and that change it. They eventually showed the PowerPoint at our school's science fair and then at the Massachusetts Institute of Technology, where they, among many others, received the 2007 Curiosity Award for their work.

All their ideas weren't correct, but they understood a significant part of how landforms begin, develop, and change. They didn't always draw the correct conclusions when they looked at a rock or at dirt or a beach, and I didn't always know the correct explanation either. But they did ask questions about what might have happened, and they knew there was history there, usually very long history, and evidence of past times. They spoke familiarly of glaciers, of erosion, of volcanoes, of vegetation, of sediment, of decomposition. They told different stories for different kinds of sand, different amounts of vegetation. They knew that they could try to imagine change and that doing this would get them far. They knew to look for cycles of change, in geology and in biology. They knew it was often useful to focus on the details: They used the scratching of a rock, the drop hitting the sand, the wave hitting the beach, the leaf slowly breaking down, in their various explanations. They knew how to make models and some of the questions to ask about them: Was it the same soil, they same sand, the same rain as in Cape Verde? Was each experimental roasting pan we made the same except for the one variable, for example, the same level of dryness of the soil?

As they wrote the text to go with their PowerPoint pictures, they also chose to mention their recognition of their fellow students' desire to know. "Our friends Paula and Djeissen had this interesting question and so our teacher said we could study it," wrote Rodolfo. He added, "We shouldn't only study America."

CHAPTER 10

Conclusion

There are many articles documenting children from underachieving groups doing exceptional work. These studies describe how the children worked and what the teachers did. They explain the children's strengths and resources and how the teachers made use of them. However, it is quite difficult to get from such accounts enough of a feel for what was done to do it yourself. We continue to bemoan the deficits and lack of understanding and knowledge of these students even though we have evidence to the contrary. As the test results come out, we marshal our resources to give them extra help on the things they don't know.

I have tried to do largely the same thing as these others, from my own perspective, the perspective of teacher research as I have learned to practice it. Teacher research, like other methods, is not a magic bullet. It will not solve all the problems. But the practices of teacher research can help to remind us that the children have plenty of knowledge—we just don't always know how to uncover it and we don't always realize immediately when it is relevant. These practices help us to remember that the children know how to think logically and effectively. They support us as we learn to provide the activities and experiences that bring this out. They are practices that help us to recognize the meaning in what all children say and think and to uncover the academic connections.

I repeat here some of the principles I have learned from doing teacher research and that I tried to keep in mind as we studied erosion in Cape Verde, as my students wondered if the sun was alive, as my students considered whether whales could possibly have been born near Haiti if they have never seen them:

1. I knew that their ideas were serious and that the more puzzling they were to me, even the more naive they sounded, the more respect and attention I had to give them. I kept a record of them, imperfect

and partial and often almost illegible, but something to help me continue to think about what they had in mind.

2. I knew that their questions were very motivating to them, and that they would lead in academic directions, whether or not they seemed important or academic to me at first. Again I kept a record.

3. I knew that for many of these students the imagination was a strong route into new knowledge and new ways of thinking. I tried to support approaches to the material we were studying that allowed them to imagine themselves inside the phenomenon.

4. I knew I had to give them the opportunity to make connections to the experiences they were familiar with, the experiences they had been thinking about in the rest of their lives outside school. I knew I might not recognize how these experiences were functioning for them at first but that academic connections would be there in time.

5. I knew that a wide range of talk, jokes, stories, reports, and arguments all contained value for their thinking and their achievement.

Teacher research contains practices that can help us, on a daily basis, to see the intellectual lives of some of our most puzzling students. I would remind us that this kind of intimacy with the ideas of thinking children is a source of great joy and of renewed energy. For most of us, it is why we entered teaching.

> Children are so powerfully attracted to the world that the very motion of their curiosity comes through to us as a form of love.
> —George Dennison, *The Lives of Children*

References

Au, K. (1980). Participation structures in a reading lesson with Hawaiian children: Analysis of a culturally appropriate instructional event. *Anthropology and Education Quarterly, 11*, 91–115.

Ballenger, C. (1999). *Regarding children's words.* New York: Teachers College Press.

Barnes, D. (1976). *From communication to curriculum.* Harmondsworth, UK: Penguin.

Berkley, P. (1994). *Science circle.* Unpublished manuscript.

Boggs. S. T. (1985). *Speaking, relating, and learning: A study of Hawaiian children at home and at school.* Norwood, NJ: Ablex.

Brookline Teacher Researcher Seminar. (2004). *Regarding children's talk: Research on languge and literacy.* New York: Teachers College Press.

Carini, P. (1979). *The art of seeing and the visibility of the person.* Grand Forks: North Dakota Study Group, University of North Dakota.

Cazden, C . (1988). *Classroom discourse: The language of teaching and learning.* Portsmouth, NH: Heinemann.

Dennison, G. (1966). *The lives of children: The story of the First Street School.* New York: Landon House.

Duckworth, E. (1987). *The having of wonderful ideas.* New York: Teachers College Press.

Foster, M. (1983). *Sharing time: A student-run speech event.* ERIC Clearinghouse on Elementary and Early Childhood Education ED 234 906.

Fox-Keller, E. (1983). *Reflections on gender and science.* New Haven, CT: Yale University Press.

Gallas, K. (1995). *Talking their way into science: Hearing children's questions and theories and responding with curricula.* New York: Teachers College Press.

Gee, J. P. (1989). The narrativization of experience in the oral style. *Journal of Education, 171*(1), 75–96.

Goswami, D., Lewis, C., Rutherford, M., Waff, D. (2008). *On teacher inquiry: Approaches to language and literacy.* New York: Teachers College Press.

Halliday, M. A. K., & Martin, J. (1993). *Writing Science: Literacy and Discursive Power.* Pittsburgh, PA: University of Pittsburgh Press.

Heath, S. B. (1983). *Ways with words.* Cambridge: Cambridge University Press.

Hudicourt-Barnes, J. (1999). Our kids can't. *Hands On! 22*(1), 4–8.

Hudicourt-Barnes, J. (2003). The use of argumentation in Haitian Creole science classrooms. *Harvard Education Review, 73*(1), 73–93.

Hudicourt-Barnes, J., Noble, T., O'Connor, M. C., Rosebery, A., Suarez, C., Warren, B., Wright, C. (2008, March). *Making sense of children's performance on achievement tests: The case of the 5th grade MC AS.* Paper presented at the American Educational Research Association Annual Meeting, New York, NY.

Hume, K. (2001). Seeing shades of gray: Developing community through science. In G. Wells (Ed.), *Action, talk, and test* (pp. 99–117). New York: Teachers College Press.

Hymes, D. (1996). *Ethnography, linguistics, narrative inequality: Toward an understanding of voice.* Bristol, PA: Taylor & Francis.

Labov, W. (1972). *Language in the inner city: Studies in the Black English Vernacular.* Philadelphia: University of Pennsylvania Press.

Lee, C. D. (1993). *Signifying as a scaffold for literary interpretation: The pedagogical implications of an African American discourse genre.* Urbana, IL: National Council of Teachers of English.

Maxwell, J. (1996). *Qualitative research design: An interactive approach.* Thousand Oaks, CA: Sage.

Michaels, S. (1981). "Sharing time: Children's narrative styles and differential access to literacy. *Language in Society, 10*, 423–442.

Michaels, S., & O'Connor, M. C. (1993). Aligning academic task and participation by revoicing: Analysis of a classroom discourse strategy. *Anthropology and Education Quarterly, 24*(4), 318–335.

Monk, S. (2005). Why would run be a speed? Artifacts of situated actions in a curriculum plan. In R. Nemirovsky, A. Rosebery, B. Warren, & J. Solomon (Eds.), *Everyday matters in mathematics and science: Studies of complex classroom events* (pp. 11–44). Mahwah, NJ: Lawrence Earlbaum Associates.

Paley, V. (1986). On listening to what children say. *Harvard Education Review, 56*(2), 122–131.

Philips, S. U. (1983). *The invisible culture: Communication in the classroom and community on the Warm Springs Indian Reservation.* White Plains, NY: Longman.

Pothier, S. (1999, July). *Listening through confusion.* Presentation to the annual Chèche Konnen Partner Seminar, Essex, MA.

Rizzuto, M. (2008). A teacher's perspective on science talks. In A. S. Rosebery & B. Warren (Eds.), *Teaching science to English language learners: Building on students' strengths* (pp. 13–20). Arlington, VA: National Science Teachers Association Press.

Rosebery, A., & Warren, B. (1998). *Boats, balloons and classroom video: Science teaching as inquiry.* Portsmouth, NH: Heineman.

Smitherman, G. (1977). *Talking and testifying: The language of Black America.* Detroit, MI: Wayne State University Press.

Sylvan, L. (1996). Getting started with science talks. In *Teachers' Perspectives on Children's Talk in Science, TERC Working Papers 2–96* (pp. 31–46). Cambridge, MA: TERC.

Van Tassell, M. A. (2001). Student inquiry in science: Asking questions, building foundations, and making connections. In G. Wells (Ed.), *Action, talk, and text* (pp. 41–59). New York: Teachers College Press.

Warren, B., Ballenger, C., Ogonowski, M., Rosebery, A., & Hudicourt-Barnes, J. (2001). Re-thinking diversity in learning science: The logic of everyday languages. *Journal of Research of Science Teaching, 38*, 529–552.

Warren, B., & Rosebery, A. (1996). "This question is just too, too easy." Perspectives from the classroom on accountability in science. In L. Schauble & R. Glaser (Ed.), *Innovations in learning: New environments for education* (pp. 97–129). Hillsdale, NJ: Erlbaum.

Index

About the Author

Cindy Ballenger is a reading specialist and occasional science teacher in Cambridge, Massachusetts. Her goal is to help a wide range of children develop a love of thinking so she can think with them.

Ever since she was a founding member of the Brookline Teacher Researcher Seminar, she has been involved in a variety of groups that promote teacher research: the International Conference of Teacher Researchers, the board of Voices from Practice at National Association for the Education of Young Children, the Spencer Foundation Practitioner Mentoring Grants. She has published one book of her own teacher research, *Teaching Other People's Chldren* (1999), and edited a volume of research for the Brookline Teacher Researcher Seminar, as well as numerous articles. She was educated at Barnard College and received her MSEd from Wheelock College. Her interest in language led her to a PhD in Applied Linguistics at Boston University. She remains deeply interested in language, culture, and the surprising and fascinating things children say.